WHO'S WILL RI...
& What's 5 Minute Guitar?

The hardest part about learning something challenging is getting on the right path and keeping persistent with it. Getting good at anything is all about **priorities.**

5 Minute Guitar was born out of my teaching philosophy which is ultimately this: "Pick your guitar up and play for just 5 minutes a day".

When you can prioritize guitar in your life - the magic begins. There will be times when you feel challenged, but when you're committed to picking up the guitar every day, you'll be able to see serious improvement. I'm going to guarantee that once you pick up your guitar for 5 minutes, you're going to want more.

Yes - basically my "5 Minute Guitar Philosophy" is based off of trickery. I'm tricking you into practicing more!

...but the "5 Minute" element doesn't stop here. You now have access to the "5 Minute Guitar" video series from CampfireGuitarStar.rocks

Inside this membership site you'll get over 4 hours of beginner, step-by-step, free content that correlates directly with this handbook. Each video is roughly 5 minutes in length and there are 5 minute practice sections throughout the series. There are so many 5 minute elements that it only made sense to title this method - "5 Minute Guitar".

So that's the story! If you work with the system, the system works. I've been teaching this method to thousands of people over the years with awesome results.

Why You Might Consider Listening To Me & Following My System

If you're like me, you want to avoid the jokers. I want to quickly tell you who I am so you can confidently spend time on this system.

I picked up the guitar when I was 9 years old. After graduating in Music Performance, Business and Technology from the Berklee College Of Music's affiliate, Selkirk College, in 2006, I started working as a pro level guitarist.

I've shared the stage with Grammy award winners and legitimate rock stars including Rev Theory, Jethro Tull's guitarist Martin Barre and David Bowie's guitarist Tony Springer. I've opened for many popular bands from Lynyrd Skynyrd to LMFAO. I've had my original compositions played on top radio stations, performed for the Olympic Games and have been featured on major television networks like MTV and MuchMusic.

During this time as a performing and studio musician, I founded the Vancouver Guitar School where myself and my team of instructors have taught all ages, levels and styles. It's been truly amazing for me to see my students becoming "real guitar players" - people who can strum chords, play songs and teach themselves their favorite songs and styles!

I'm genuinely excited to share my knowledge, and dedicated to creating systems that help each student achieve their dream of playing music. It is with this foundation that "5 Minute Guitar" was born.

Will This System Work For Me?

The 5 Minute Guitar system is a powerful solution if you want to learn the important fundamentals, get playing, get strumming and start having a blast... and for little or no investment cash wise! The information is laid out in exciting videos and jam tracks, plus a wealth of bonus material that can be found online and within this book... but I'll be honest, a big part of the puzzle could be missing. Could "5 Minute Guitar" be broken?

The one big thing missing is the interaction and guidance by a real person in real time. If this book and video series don't absolutely get you 'rockin' the house', it's possible that videos and books just aren't the best way for you to learn.

You see, everyone has a different learning "modality". Some people like to read and learn, some people like to watch and learn and some people like to be shown how. Often, a combination of these "modalities" works the best!

You don't have to invest your time and money with my company but certainly, me and my team at Campfire Guitar Star have powerful solutions for 1-on-1 lessons. We teach people nearly every single day from all over the world. As I'm writing, I'm based in Canada and I've taught students via webcam in Japan, Israel, New Zealand, England, Brazil and all over the US and Canada.

I'm going to guess that you're someone who wants to be committed, get a solid grasp on guitar concepts and have fun playing - working with a pro, fun instructor could be the missing piece of the puzzle to achieve that next level of guitar playing.

Yes! You should consider working with a real person in real time at some point in your guitar playing!

Rip It Up!

I truly hope you experience the results you're after. I am so passionate about the guitar and am here to help get music into people's lives in a big way.

Let's get started! Dial up those videos and follow along in the book and we'll start rippin' it up!

Will Ripley

Apply For 1-on-1 Guitar Lessons Here:
http://www.CampfireGuitarStar.com/1on1coaching

Get Access to the Videos Here:
http://www.CampfireGuitarStar.Rocks

Rather Connect By Phone? Call us:
1-855-974-7539

MAKE MONEY WITH YOUR GUITAR

Teach Beginners How To Play The Guitar

QUIT YOUR DAY JOB & MAKE UP TO $5,000 A MONTH
(While only working 20 hours a week)

Will Ripley's

GUITAR INSTRUCTOR ALLIANCE

Get access to a full, A-Z business building course that covers everything a new guitar instructor would need to know.

Discover how to get students, how to teach guitar & how to create a powerful, online presence that will ensure a steady stream of money…for doing what you love!

Sign Up For The "Guitar Instructor Blueprint" & Free Training Videos at:
WWW.WILLRIPLEY.COM/TEACHERSTOOLS

5 MINUTE GUITAR SYSTEM

Copyright 2016 © Will Ripley
All Rights Reserved

DON'T LIMIT YOURSELF
Login & Get All The Videos!

This Book Corresponds Directly To The Video Series. Improve Your Likelihood Of Guitar Success By Combining The Written Material & The Step-By-Step Video Instruction!

Register and Login At:
WWW.CAMPFIREGUITARSTAR.ROCKS

TABLE OF CONTENTS

MODULE 1: CRASH COURSE

Chapter 1: Starting Out Right With Your First Guitar Lesson Ever — 2
Looking Deeper Into Sounds & Strings — 6
Chapter 2: Super Easy Guitar Tablature For Beginners - Your First Riff Ever — 10
Chapter 3: 100% Correct Guitar Technique - Eliminate Bad Habits For Good! — 14

MODULE 2: SUPER SIMPLE FUN RIFFS

Chapter 4: Seven Nation Army — 26
Chapter 5: I Love Rock N' Roll — 28
Chapter 6: Comes As Your Are — 31
Chapter 7: Born Under A Bad Sign — 33
Chapter 8: Hey Joe — 36
Discovering Your Natural Motivation - Get A Great Practice Routine — 38

MODULE 3: MUST KNOW SCALES

Chapter 9: The Major Scale & Scale Charts — 44
Chapter 10: Power Chords & Intervals - Simple & Powerful Rock Guitar Techniques — 47
Chapter 11: Pentatonic Scales - Must Know Scales — 50

MODULE 4: POWER CHORD ROCK SONGS

Chapter 12: Confused By Tab? Discover The Secrets Of Tablature — 54
Guitar Tablature Legend — 56
Chapter 13: Iron Man — 57
Chapter 14: 21 Guns — 59
Chapter 15: Rock Guitar Techniques Using Power Chords — 60
Chapter 16: Power Chord Graduation - I Love Rock N' Roll — 62

MODULE 5: MASTER GUITAR CHORDS

- **Chapter 17:** Chord Charts - Learn To Play Any Chord (Start With This One) — 66
- **Chapter 18:** Easy Chords For Beginners - The Best Chords To Learn FIRST — 71
- **Chapter 19:** Awesome Beginner Strumming Songs — 76
- **Chapter 20:** Part 2 - Awesome Beginner Strumming Songs — 78
- **Chapter 21:** How To Stick Chords Quickly & Remember Them Forever — 82
- What Every Great Guitarist In History Has Done & Why You Might Consider Doing It Too — 84
- **Chapter 22:** Paradise City — 91
- **Chapter 23:** Free Fallin' — 93
- **Chapter 24:** Sweet Child O' Mine — 94
- **Chapter 25:** Leaving On A Jet Plane — 97

MODULE 6: BARRE CHORDS: PLAY EVERY MAJOR + MINOR CHORD

- **Chapter 26:** Discover Every Note On The Guitar Fretboard (Unlock The Grid) — 102
- **Chapter 27:** Intro To Barre Chords — 106
- Tips On Playing Barre Chords — 108
- **Chapter 28:** Master 2 "E-String" Bare Chord Shapes — 113
- **Chapter 29:** Master 2 "A-String" Barre Chord Shapes — 117
- **Chapter 30:** Barre Chords Mastery Song Lesson - "Creep" — 120
- **Chapter 31:** Part 2 - Barre Chords Mastery Song Lesson — 123

BONUS MATERIALS/REFERENCE

- Parts Of The Guitar — 128
- Chords — 129
- Changing Your Strings — 134
- Tips On Buying A Guitar — 140

EPILOGUE

- **Chapter 32:** Final Lesson & Will's Advice — 146

MODULE 1

CRASH COURSE

CHAPTER 1

STARTING OUT RIGHT
WITH YOUR FIRST GUITAR LESSON EVER

Getting Started

Having your guitar properly set up will keep it in top shape, and allow you to play easier, faster and longer.

First, we are going to check out "The Action" of the strings. If this isn't setup correctly, it can hold a beginner back from ever experiencing success on the guitar.

The "action" of the guitar refers to the height of the strings off of the neck and body. If your guitar has "high action", it will make it very difficult to press your fingers down and get a clean note. While some advanced players enjoy setting up and fine tuning their instrument, this can be a difficult task and it's recommended you save this type of work for professional guitar builders and repair people who are titled "Luthiers".

Here are some reasons you might want to consider consulting with a Luthier:

1. If your strings are high off the fretboard (aka "your guitar has high action")
2. If your notes sound buzzy
3. If your guitar won't stay in tune
4. If you find notes hard to fret
5. You have bought a new guitar (often guitar stores offer a "free setup")

Tuning

The first thing you do when you pick up your guitar, is tune it. Tuning involves the tightening or loosening of each string to achieve the desired pitch or note. No matter how good you are at the guitar, if you're out of tune, just going to sound bad. This is not "Guitar Hero", this is a live instrument. Lack of use, extended use, and changes the environment all have an affect on the tuning.
A soft touch with an element of 'feel' will become skill you will master over time.

Universal APP
Designed for both iPhone and iPad

Will Ripley Tuner

If you don't have a tuner, buy a tuner. If you have an iPhone or iPad, head over to the Apple App store, search "Will Ripley" and for $2.99 you can download my tuner! It works with the built-in microphone, is extremely accurate and has over 100 tuning modes so you can use it for a bass, ukulele or even a banjo. Now you'll always have an easy to use tuner with you wherever you go!

Now! The fastest and most effective way to tune your guitar:

1. Start with the fattest string, this is also referred to as your 'lowest string' or 'low E string"
2. Doing your best to mute the other strings while you repeatedly hit the string, keeping your eyes on the tuner
3. Now ask yourself, "Do I need to tighten or loosen the string?"
4. Simultaneously turn the tuning peg to achieve the pitch you're looking for

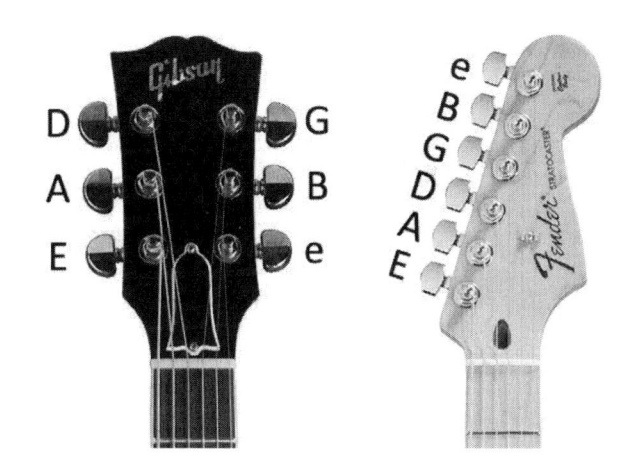

*You will get used to the feel of the strings. Sometimes they need the smallest touch up, and sometimes they need to fall a bit flat in order to stretch to the desired pitch.

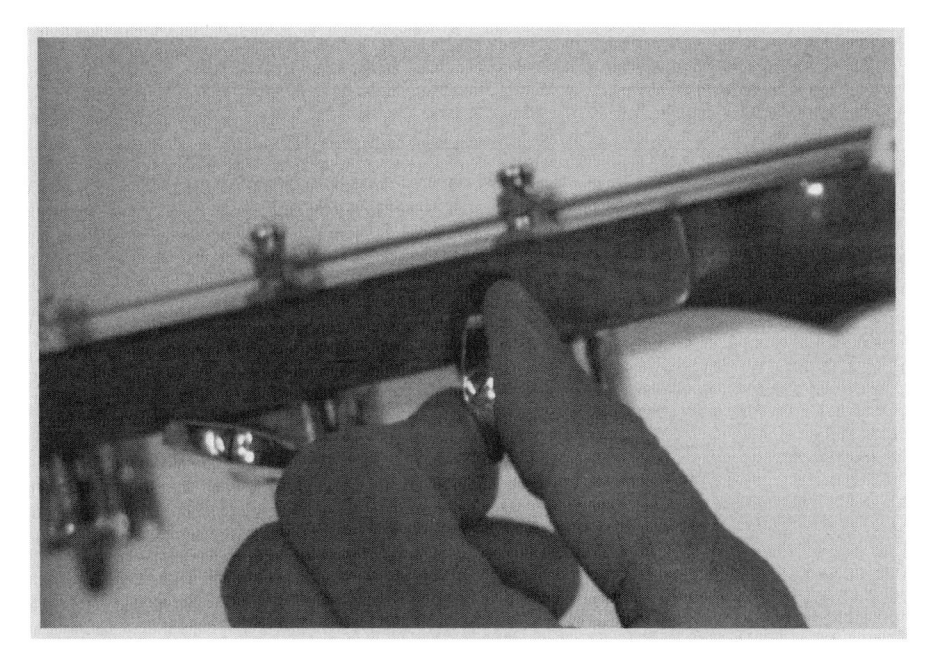

Now that you have progressively tuned all the strings, go through them again. Remember when I said your guitar was a "live instrument"? The change in pressure on each string will both relax and have an effect the other strings. Wood is surprisingly flexible.

This may sound daunting and tedious but don't worry, when practiced, the process will go very fast and make you sound in tune. Trust me, it's worth every second!

Congratulations on taking the most important, very first steps to playing guitar! Your guitar is set-up, tuned and ready to be played. Now let's learn how to play this thing!

LOOKING DEEPER
INTO SOUNDS & STRINGS

Let's face it, things sound a lot better when they're in tune!

A music conference took place in 1939, and these music peeps decided that "concert pitch" (Or their reference point when tuning) was going to be the "A" note that registered at 440hz.

This way, when massive orchestras would get together and rock out, they would all have some sort of reference.

The first standardized tuners were these U shaped pieces of metal that resonate at a specific frequency (or pitch). Many instruments at that time projected sound from their own body, so you could tap the metal bar on something and then place the end of it against the body of your instrument to amplify the note. Soon after came the electric strobe tuner, these are still very popular today and remain extremely accurate. Check out the company Peterson, they make excellent strobe tuners!

So let's get to the GUITAR now. We have an A string that's calibrated to 440hz for sure! it's the second biggest string on the guitar.

Going from big to small, we have E, A, D, G, B, and little e. Everything from classical to hard rock can share the same tuning across 6 strings. It's pretty cool!

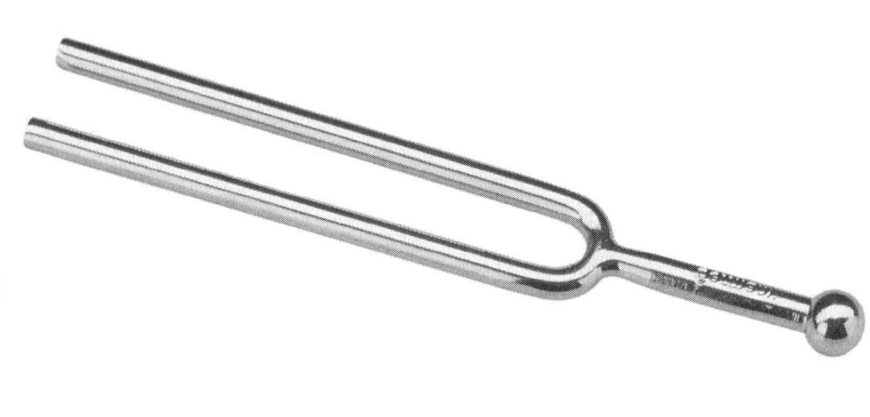

Although there are so many different ways to tune your guitar, we shouldn't feel limited. Great bands like The Rolling Stones and Big Wreck have almost all of their songs in altered tunings. It's a very common thing. Also, more current pop acts like John Mayer and The Goo Goo Dolls are well known for their unstandardized tunings!

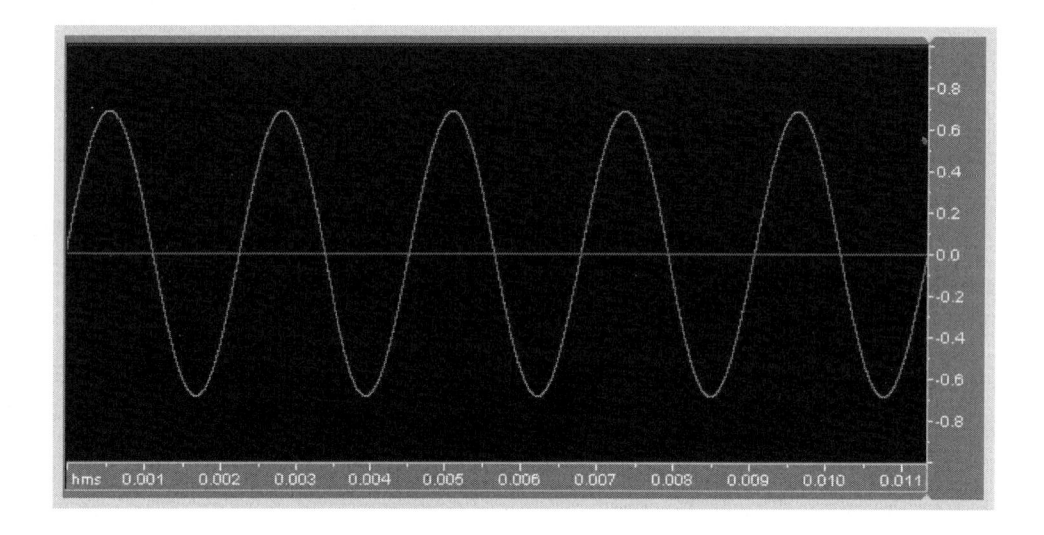

The argument is "IS 440 THE MOST MUSICAL FREQUENCY?" I'm going to do more investigation on this and get back to you. There are many types of music related therapy, meditation and science behind the different frequencies, what they do, how they affect us. It's really fascinating and when you think of it. There's something about music and how different songs and genres make us feel just by being exposed to these different frequencies.

If you're looking for a tuner and own an iPhone, iPad or iPod you can download the Will Ripley Guitar Tuner from the App store. Just search for "Will Ripley" in the App store and you'll find it. It's really accurate and easy to use. I use this tuner in a free video titled "How To Tune Your Guitar". It will teach you tricks and tips on how to tune your guitar effectively.

Playing an in-tune guitar separates a good sound from a bad sound.

If you were to pass a totally out of tune to any amazing guitarist, they will sound horrible. So, if you want a huge tip that will INSTANTLY make you sound more pro, get your guitar perfectly in tune.

It takes a bit of practice to know how to get your guitar into perfect tune, but the WR tuner would really help and you can watch my lesson on how to tune your guitar (I use the iPhone app in the video so you can learn how to use it as well as tune your guitar).

Universal APP
Designed for both iPhone and iPad

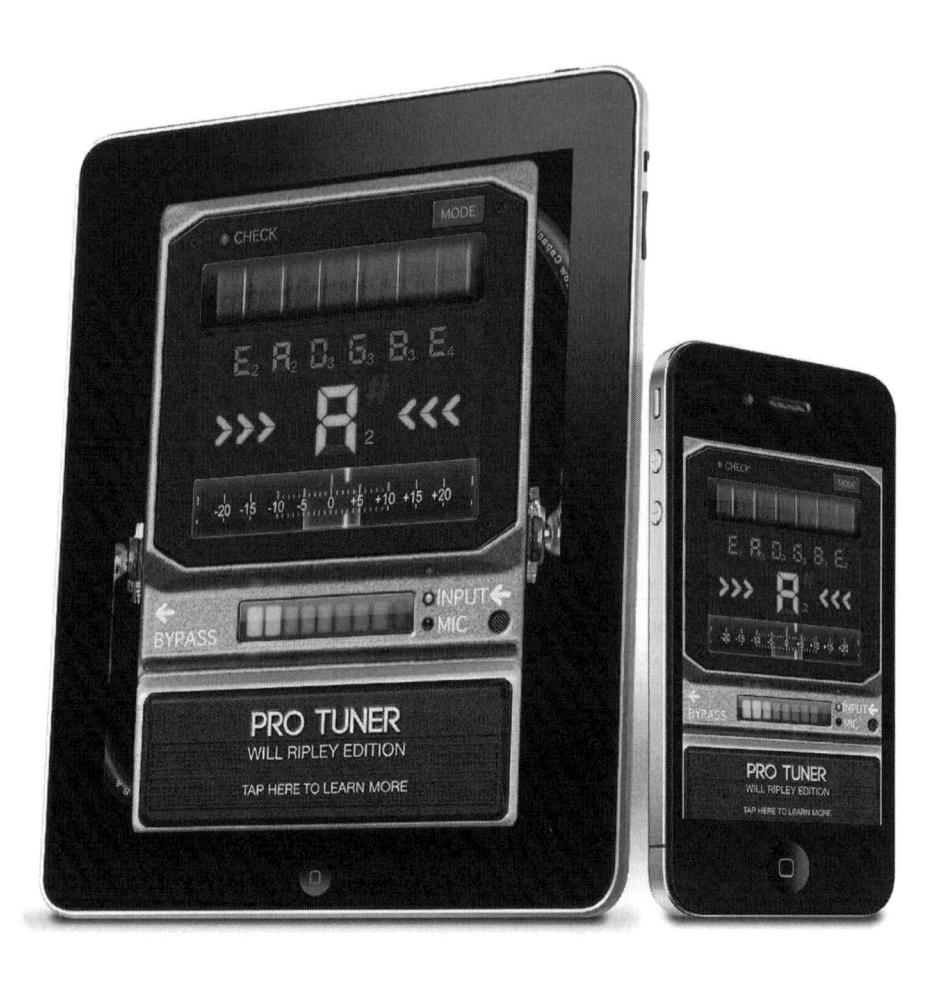

TUNE UP!

GET THE WILL RIPLEY PRO TUNER

*Just search 'Will Ripley' in the App Store

CHAPTER 2

SUPER EASY GUITAR TABLATURE FOR BEGINNERS - YOUR FIRST RIFF EVER

Reading tab

We have a guitar that is set up, in tune, we know the names of the strings - It's time to rock & roll! I'm going to show you a riff and we're also going to learn how to read tab.

*Tablature (or "tab" for short) - is a form of musical notation for stringed instruments. It's far from perfect because most tab doesn't show you which fingers to use or what rhythms to play - but it does tell you what notes to play and in what order!

Things to Know

```
e|------------------------------------------|
B|------------------------------------------|
G|------------------------------------------|
D|------------------------------------------|
A|------------------------------------------|
E|------------------------------------------|
```

1. Tab shows you **exactly** what notes/frets to play and in what order to play them - it's a very powerful tool to have as a guitarist.
2. Each line represents each string (6 lines on tab and there are 6 strings!)
3. (E - A - D - G - B - e) - The capital letters and lowercase letters will help you know which is the "big" string and which is the "little" string.
4. "0" represents playing an open string. You can think of the letter "o" for "open"
5. Tab tells us the sequence of the song/riff and we read it left to right (just like reading a book!)
6. The low E string (biggest string) is the bottom line of a tab diagram. It may seem like you're reading tab like your guitar is "upside down and backwards"
7. The numbers on the lines represent the frets (The frets are the raised metal strips on the fingerboard). The numbers don't have anything to do with your fingers. The numbers tell you exactly **where** to put your fingers!
8. Tab does not show you which fingers to use. You have to use common sense and your best judgement when placing your fingers on the guitar. Try to find the most "economical" way to place your fingers when reading tab so you utilize **ALL** your necessary fingers. (Many beginners are inclined to only use 1 finger for riffs)

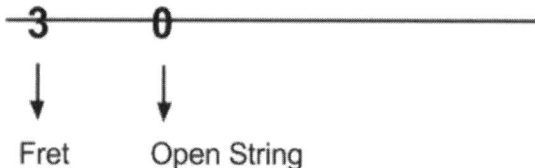

Tab may be written as if you're holding your guitar "upside down and backwards"!

Tab Combined With Musical Notation:

In professional music publications, and in the back of guitar magazines, you will often see notes or rhythmic notation in conjunction with tab. This takes tab a step closer to being "perfect" because a person that has the ability to read music can be hugely assisted with the rhythmic placement of the notes.

Here's an example of the C Major scale written out in tab with accompanying musical notation. The time signature, found on the left, is 4/4, so each black note gets one beat. The last note, pictured with the open center, means it gets 2 beats, completing the bar.

C Major Scale (Open Position)

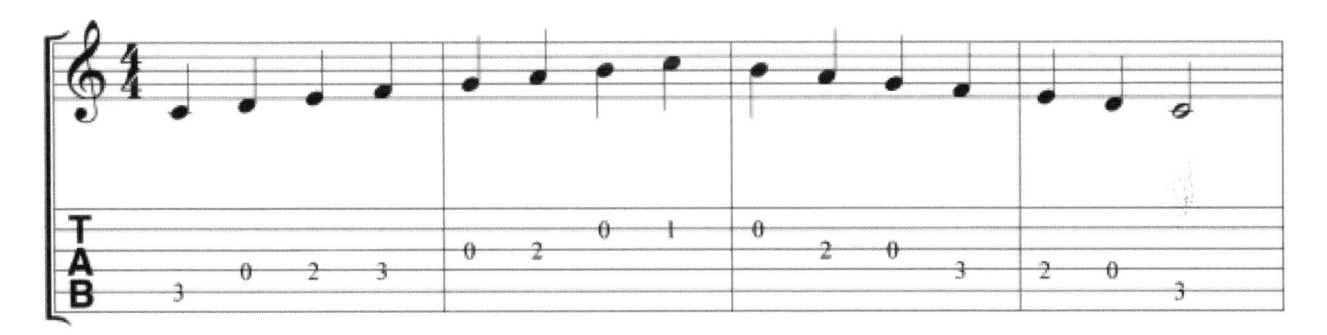

Smoke On The Water - A Great "First Riff" For A Beginner Guitar Player

"Smoke on the Water" was written and released by Deep Purple in 1972. The famous riff was played on a Fender Stratocaster by guitar legend, Ritchie Blackmore.

It's also known as "the first song you learn on guitar". We're going to stay true to that tradition and get you having some fun right off the bat!

To start off, we're going to learn this song as a "bass line" or a "single-note riff" on the guitar. The actual song is played in a different key and utilizes 2 strings at the same time so this is a beginner version.

Tips On Playing This Riff:

1. Look up "Smoke on the Water - Deep Purple" and have a listen so you can become familiar with the riff. This will help you play it so it doesn't sound like random notes.
2. Read the notes, one at a time, left to right.
3. When placing the tips of your fingers on the frets, play very close to the frets (play right "above" the fret). This will help eliminate unwanted fret buzz.
4. Bonus Tip - Once you master the riff on the low E string, try out the same riff on each one of the 6 strings. This will "transpose" the riff into a different key and give you some practice playing on different strings.

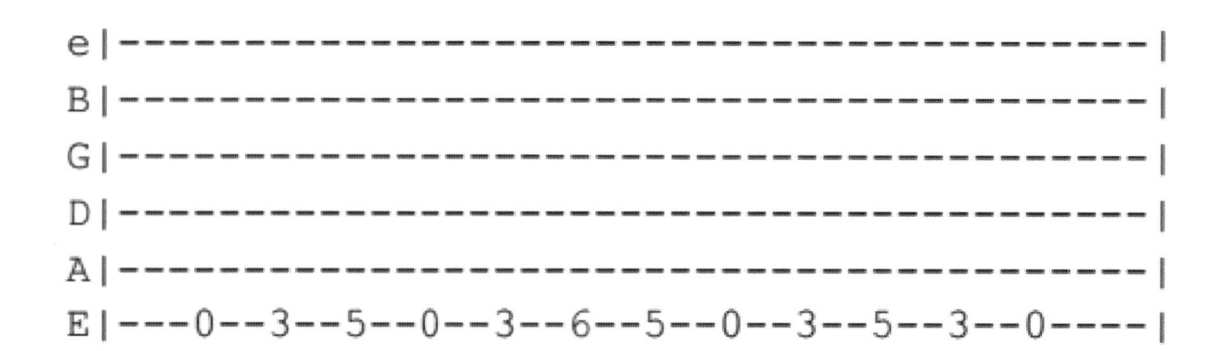

```
e|----------------------------------------|
B|----------------------------------------|
G|----------------------------------------|
D|----------------------------------------|
A|----------------------------------------|
E|---0--3--5--0--3--6--5--0--3--5--3--0---|
```

Congrats on your very first guitar riff!

CHAPTER 3

100% CORRECT GUITAR TECHNIQUE
- ELIMINATE BAD HABITS FOR GOOD!

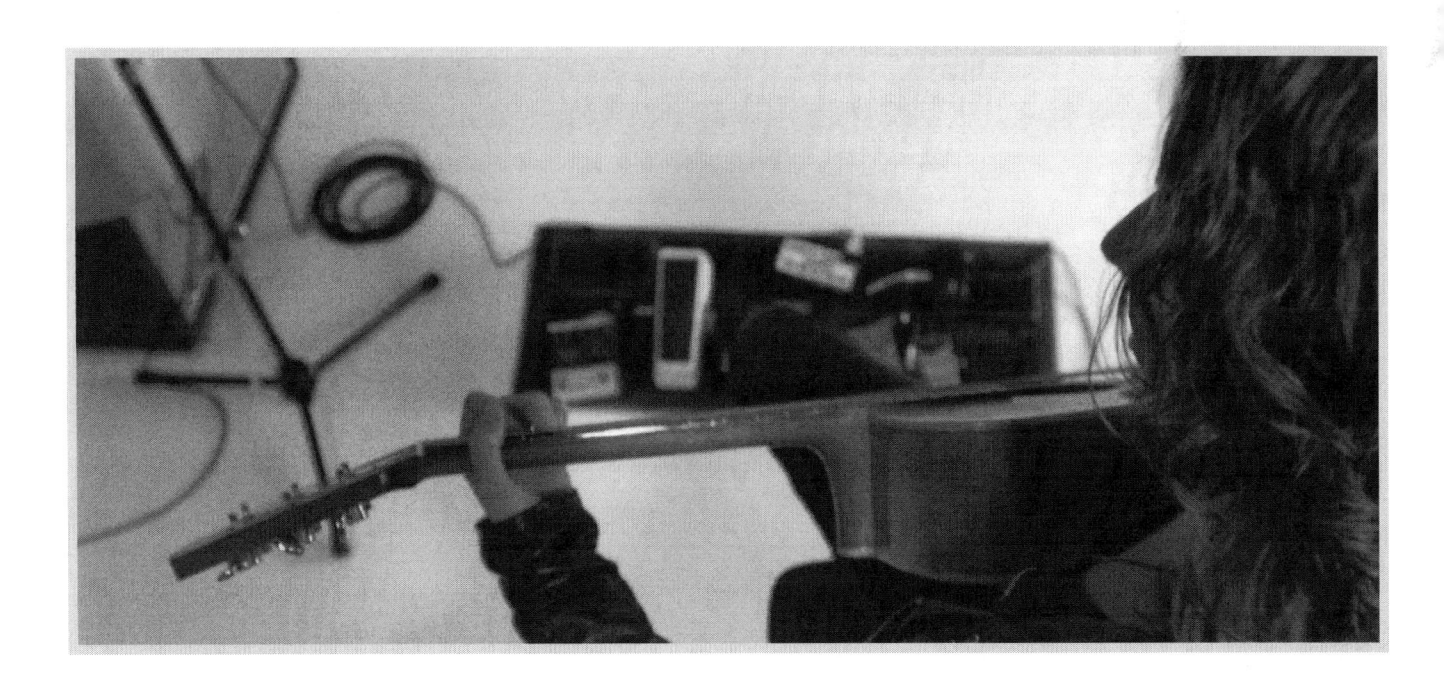

Before we continue playing awesome riffs, I want to make sure your left and your right hand techniques are dialled in.

Technique #1 How To Rest The Guitar In Your Lap For Years Of Comfortable Playing

1. Sitting in an upright position, resting the guitar on your leg, hold the guitar close to your body, with the neck of the guitar pointing straight (not dipping or raising by too much)
2. Slide the guitar away from you by 1-2 inches
3. Tilt the guitar back into your chest so you can clearly see the fretboard while maintaining a comfortable position (try not to hunch or curve your back over the guitar)
4. Make sure your right leg is high enough - Use a support to raise your right leg if needed. This could be anything from a block, to your chairs cross brace, to a dedicated guitar foot stool
5. Sit back and relax! Remember, you won't become a better guitar player with your face close to the fret board. Sit back in your chair and use the backrest for extra support

Technique #2 The Buzz Test - How To Get Crystal Clear Notes!

Placing your fingers on different areas of the same fret will have a huge impact on how you sound. Playing notes while snugged right up behind the fret you're playing will give you the best and clearest sound. Without this simple tweak, a guitarist may sound like a rookie forever!

The buzz test can also show you how little pressure is actually needed when fretting a note! Another step towards making the guitar as stress-free and easy as it can be.

Put Yourself Through The Buzz Test:

1. Find the 3rd fret on the low E (the 3rd metal bar on the thickest string)

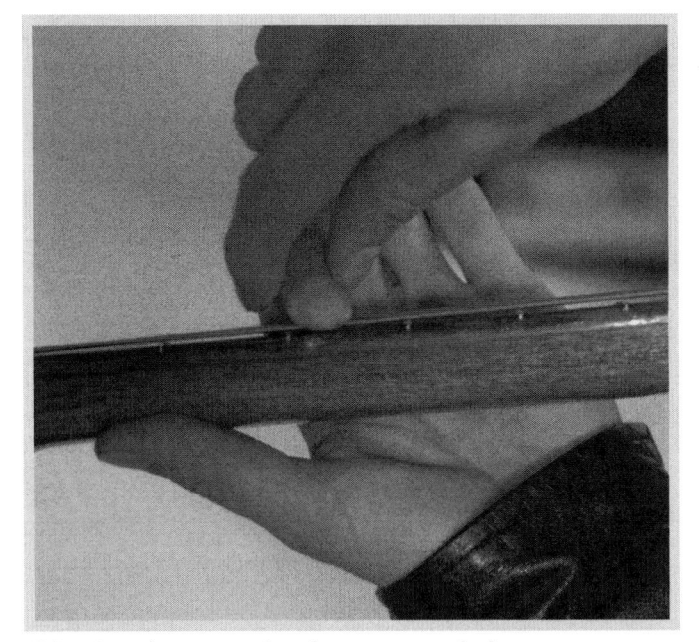

Playing low on the frets sounds buzzy 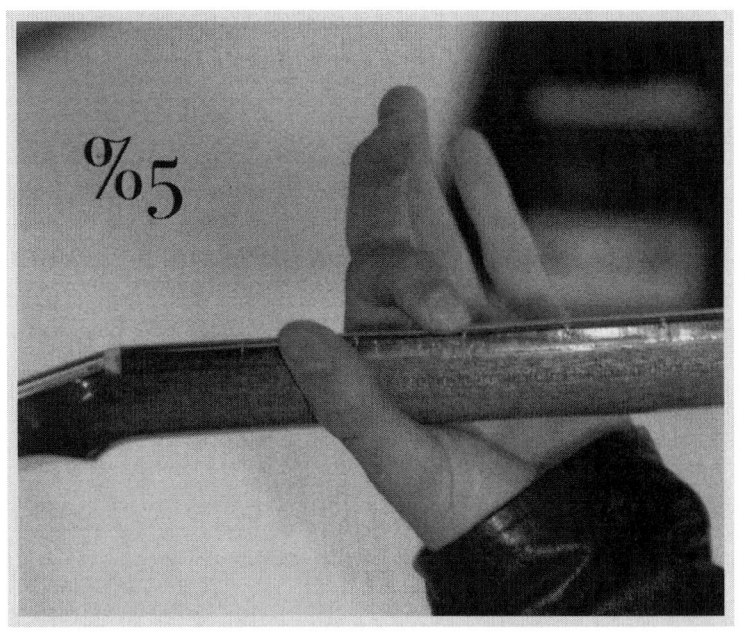   *Playing close to the fret sounds clear!*

2. Now try this - Move your finger as LOW as you can in the "fret zone" and play as far away from the 3rd fret as you can (fret your finger close to the 2nd fret). Strike the string with your right hand. It probably sounds buzzy - if it doesn't, intentionally apply a low amount of pressure with your left hand to get that nasty buzzy sound. Sounds brutal, right?

3. Now move your finger right up to the 3rd fret (as close as you possibly can without being on top of the fret) and play the string again. Is it clear? YES!

4. If you complete the buzz test and you're still getting buzz, try pushing just 5% harder to access that clean, clear note!

The buzz test is designed for you to understand why you might be getting a buzzing sound from the strings while you play and how to eliminate it forever.

If you're STILL getting buzz, there's probably something wrong with your guitar. To eliminate the buzz from the guitar, it would need to be looked over by a luthier (more on Luthiers in Chapter 1).

(Please note, that it's normal for electric guitars to have a little bit of buzz. As long as it's not coming through the amp and restricting the guitars ability to sustain notes, then that's ok!)

Technique #3 The "Warm Up Scale" - The Movement That Pro's Use & Beginners Can Do Easily

The "warm up scale" involves simply going up and down the frets and strings, one at a time. This is a great way to warm up and practice; beginners play it, professionals play it.

*Remember to keep your fingers high up on the frets and your thumb planted on the back of the neck. It will look and sound like a straightforward 1-2-3-4.

1. Start with your first finger on the 3rd fret of the low E string and play that note (tip: you can actually play this anywhere, but in this example we're using the 3rd fret).
2. Continue by playing the same string now with your second finger on the 4th fret.
3. Then third finger on the 5th fret.
4. Then fourth finger on the 6th fret.
5. Now move up to your "A" string and in the same place repeat that 1,2,3,4.
6. Continue on each string, all the way up to your high "e" string.

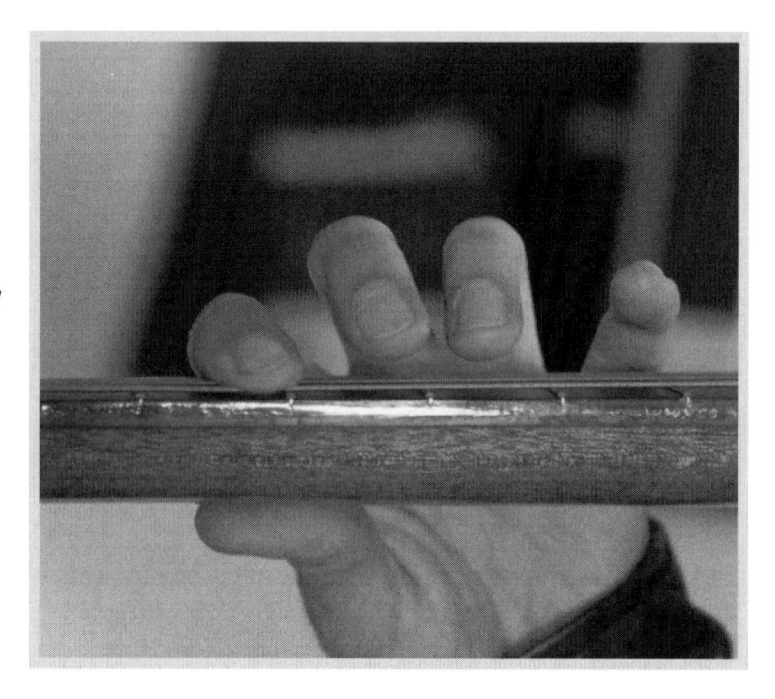

```
e|---------------------------------------3-4-5-6--
B|-----------------------------3-4-5-6------------
G|---------------------3-4-5-6--------------------
D|-------------3-4-5-6----------------------------
A|-----3-4-5-6------------------------------------
E|3-4-5-6-----------------------------------------
```

After you have tried going up, see if you can do the same thing in reverse and go back down. If you get bored, try moving up one fret after each rotation. You win the warm up scale by playing every note from the bottom to the top and back down (this includes the open strings)... but seriously, you win because you are now warmed up!

When playing ANY scale (including our warm up scale) here's your priority list. Notice that "#3. Speed" get's the bronze medal - it's still important and makes the podium, but isn't as important as #1. Clear Notes and #2. Consistency/Rhythm

#1. Clear Notes

#2 Consistency

#3 Speed

Technique #4 - How To Have Total Control Over The Guitar & How Pro's Play With Their Eyes Closed

Your Right Hand

Your right hand is a huge part of your sound and control on the guitar. The first things to consider are your stabilization points. As you can see from this picture, there are no stability points in place. In this position, a guitar player's hand is essentially "floating".

Now we're sitting straight, with an arm comfortably over the guitar, playing some notes, we're going to install these "must-know" techniques into your playing which will basically ensure your success on the instrument.

"The Thumb Pillow"

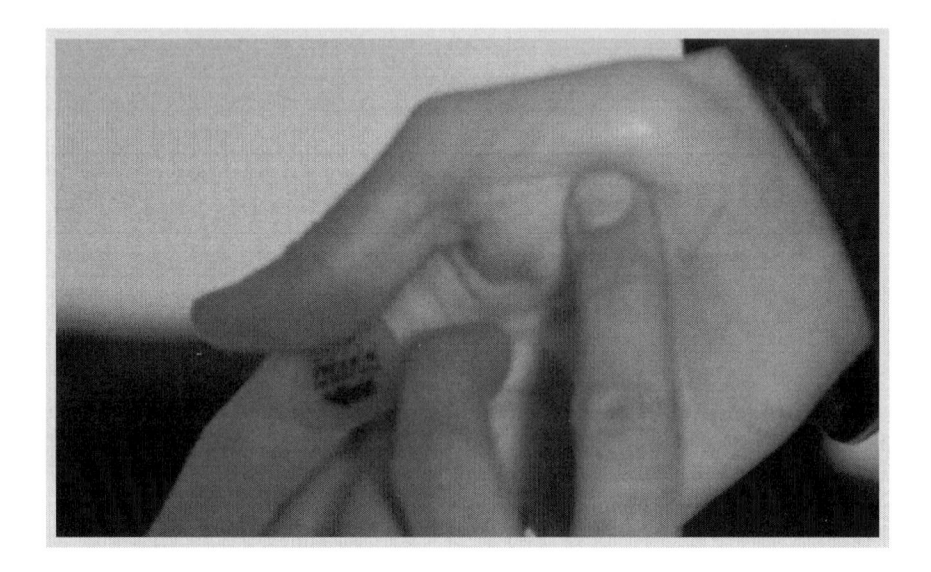

The thumb pillow is on the palm of your hand, just down from your thumb. It's that fleshy part, and one of your most important contact points with the strings. What you're going to do is rest your thumb pillow on the strings OR the bridge. If you're playing notes on your A string for example, try resting your thumb pillow on the E string just above it.

The middle of your wrist at the base of your palm often sits on the bridge of the guitar. This provides a great stability point and gets your hand in a good position to play.

Keeping your wrist angle straight, try playing your warm up scale, one note at a time while using the thumb pillow. You'll notice that you will naturally be moving your hand across the strings/bridge as you go up or down the scale. This will also keep all of the strings that you are not playing, from making sounds.

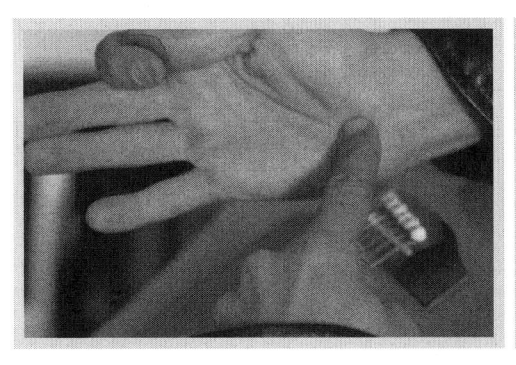

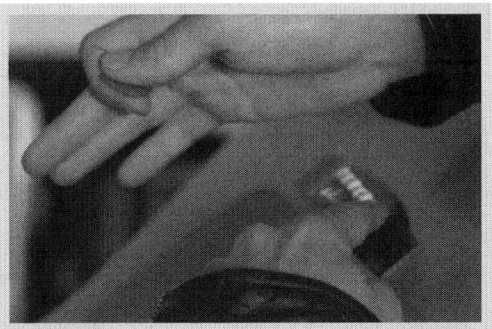

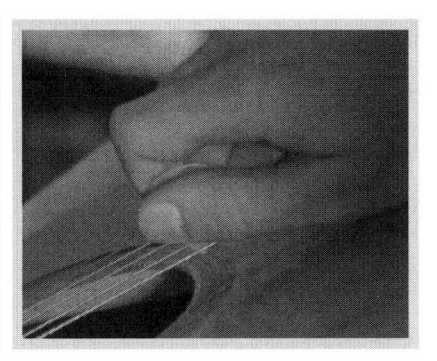

Learning these techniques from the very beginning is the secret to playing great songs note for note.

Technique #5 - The Pick - What To Use & How To Hold It To Play Faster And Smoother

A pick can be anything that's used in the playing of a stringed instrument. People in the 1900's used wood, metal, whatever! Famous guitarists have recorded with coins or even cut up credit cards!

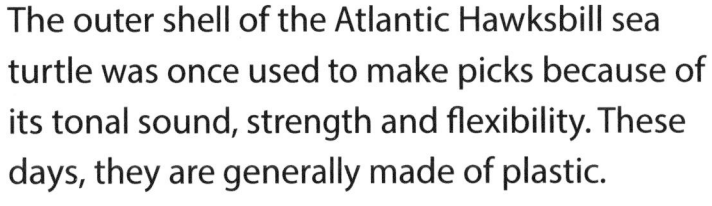

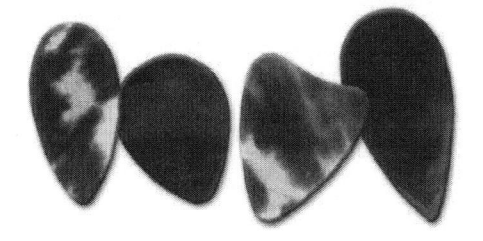

The outer shell of the Atlantic Hawksbill sea turtle was once used to make picks because of its tonal sound, strength and flexibility. These days, they are generally made of plastic.

Picks are usually referred to by thickness in millimeters. A heavier pick generally produces a darker, louder sound. I recommend that beginner guitar players use a .73mm thick pick (or close to).

Learning how to hold your pick properly, and choosing one that feels/sounds right, will enable you to get the best sound out of your guitar.

20

Holding The Pick:

- Hold the pick out so the tip comes to the end of your first finger.

- Let your thumb fall naturally on top of the pick to hold it down.

- Curl your index finger in behind it and leave the tip out just past your thumb.

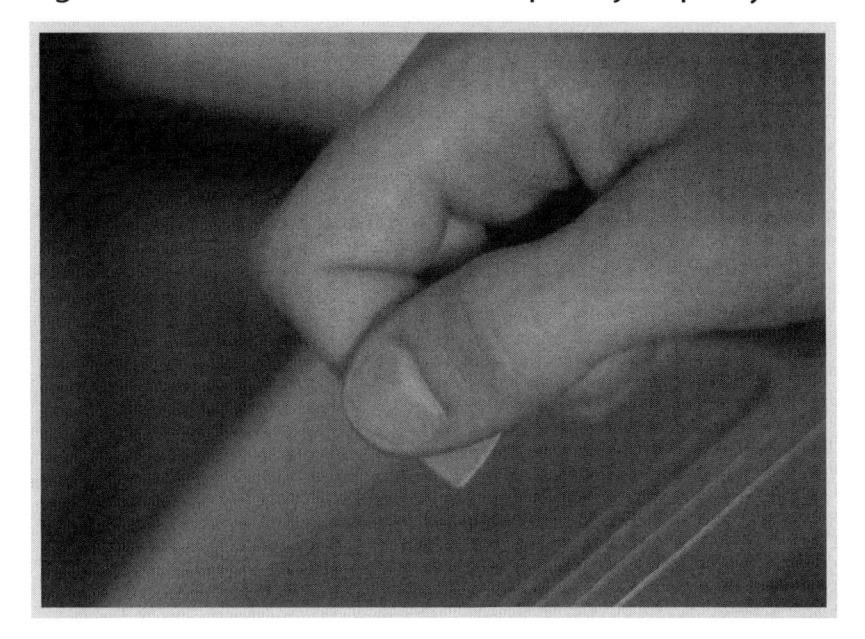

Technique #6 - The Secret To Playing Fast - The 45* Pick Angle

This techniques I'm sharing with you should naturally put the pick on a 45 degree angle. This reduces the amount of contact the pick has with the strings. You're going to be able to play faster and smoother!

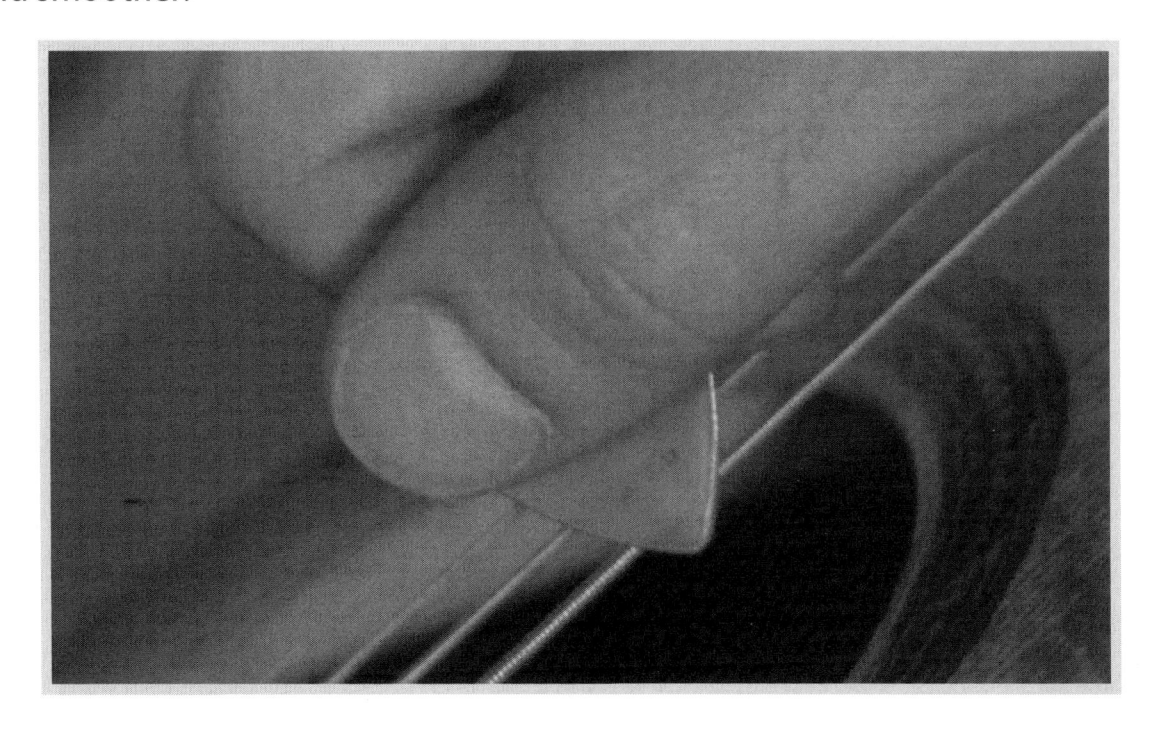

Technique Summary

If you've already been playing guitar for awhile, allow this chapter to be a big "reset button". If you're a brand new beginner, don't overlook these techniques! In my many years of teaching experience - guitarists will ultimately be held back without these techniques in place.

By the way! This isn't stuff that I'm making up. The material you'll find here is what famous guitar players do from Slash, to Zakk Wylde to Paul Mccartney.

The warm-up scale (1,2,3,4 scale) is great to use when first applying these techniques. Because of it's simplicity, you can focus on all your elements of 100% correct, left and right hand technique.

Let's keep on rippin'!

LET PEOPLE KNOW WHO YOU ARE AND WHAT YOU DO!

Let Everyone Know You're A **"Campfire Guitar Star"**

Get t-shirts and more at
WWW.CAMPFIREGUITARSTAR.COM/MERCH

MODULE 2

SUPER SIMPLE FUN RIFFS

CHAPTER 4

SEVEN NATION ARMY

Seven Nation Army

The White Stripes had a chart topping hit with "Seven Nation Army" back in 2003. After weeks at #1 it went on to win the Grammy Award for best rock song of that year. Jack White's guitar sound was fundamental to the band as they performed only as a 2 piece (drums/guitar/vocals).

For the famous riff, Jack used a vintage Kay guitar through a pedal called a "DigiTech Whammy". This pedal was used to move the pitch down exactly one octave while the hollow-body of the guitar produced a more rounded tone. The result is a unique 'bass like' guitar riff. This song as been the protest song for Egypt in 2011 and the anthem of Italy's World Cup win in 2006 as well as countless other sporting events, movies, tv shows and video games… and it's just 5 notes!

When I teach this song to my students, I transpose the key to "A". The original version is in E. If you don't have the DigiTech Whammy pedal, it sounds a bit better like this.

7 NATION ARMY

```
e|------------------------------------------------|
B|------------------------------------------------|
G|------------------------------------------------|
D|------------------------------------------------|
A|-----------3------------------------------------|
E|--5----5-------5----3----1----0-----------------|
```

Getting Ready

1. Look up "Seven Nation Army - White Stripes" on the internet and have a listen.
2. Become familiar enough with the riff so you can hum along in real time.
3. Read the tab, play the notes and see how close you can come to nailing the riff!

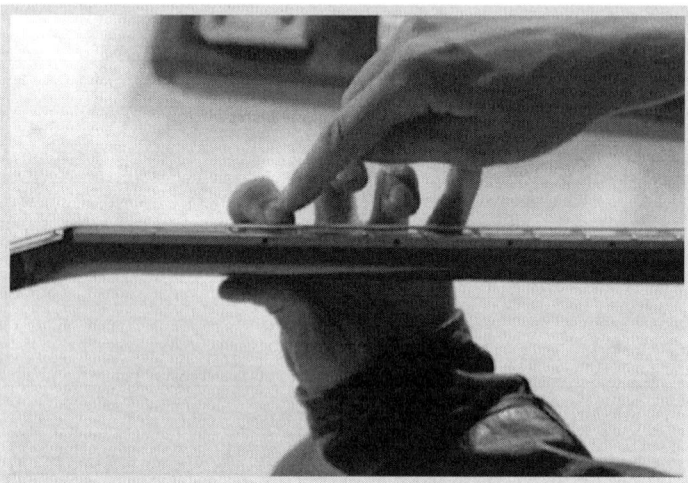

Start by playing the 5th fret of the E string with your 3rd finger. This will get your hand into the perfect position to play that 3rd fret of your A string with your 1st finger.

To complete the riff continue to move your hand down, playing the third and first frets with your first finger.

* Sit up straight & remember proper technique.
* Find the rhythm with your body. Tap your toe, dance a little bit in your chair etc. This will help you stay on beat and play with more feel.

CHAPTER 5

I LOVE ROCK & ROLL

I Love Rock & Roll

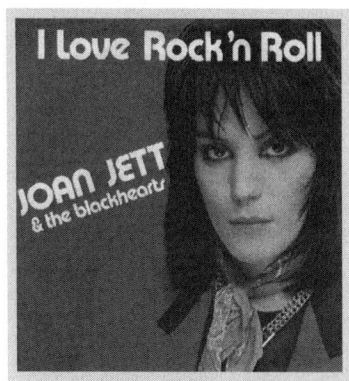

Originally written and released as a B-side in 1975 by a band called "The Arrows", "I Love Rock & Roll" didn't reach its peak in popularity until it was covered by Joan Jett and her band "The Blackhearts" in 1982. It spent seven weeks at #1 on the US billboard, ranked #89 on Rolling Stones "100 Greatest Guitar Songs" and was inducted into the Grammy's Hall of Fame in 2006. Not bad for a cover!

Getting ready

1. Look up "I love Rock & Roll" on the internet and have a listen.
2. Get familiar with the riff so you can hum along in real time.

I LOVE ROCK N' ROLL

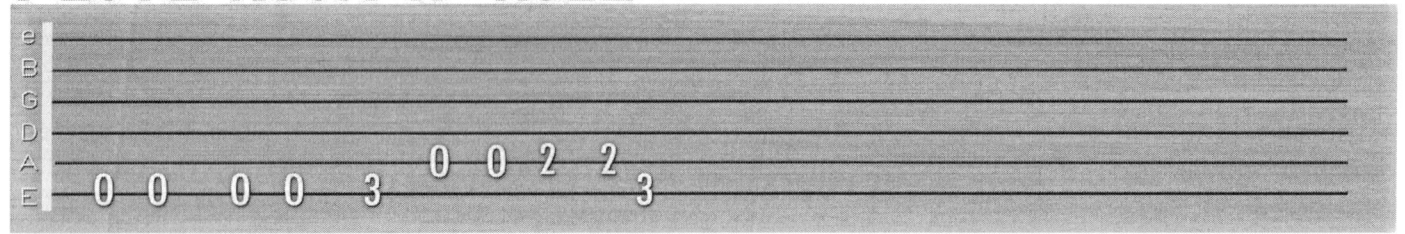

```
e|----------------------------------------
B|----------------------------------------
G|----------------------------------------
D|----------------------------------------
A|-------------------0--0--2--2-----------
E|-0--0----0--0--3------------3-----------
```

It's just as simple as listening to the song, reading the tab and nailing it. However, you might notice that it sounds a bit different than the original recording. That's because we're playing it as a bassline/single-note riff. We'll progress you to the next level very soon! Remember that for now, these riffs are essentially disguised because they're really great finger exercises.

Introducing: A New Rhythmic Technique

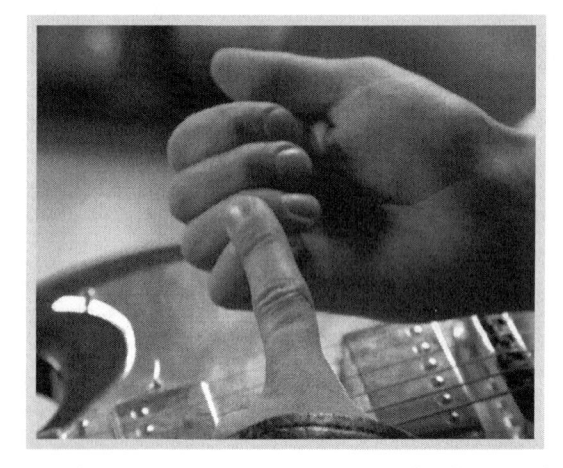

We're going to use a special technique that is used to emulate the sound of a snare drum. Holding your pick in the correct position, curl the remaining fingers into a very loose fist.

Looking at the tab, you'll see we're starting with the low E string and playing it in the open position. After playing the 2 open notes, swing that loose fist down onto the strings. It will stop the note from ringing and give you a 'clap' sound. This is the strings clanging into the frets, giving us an essential rhythmic guitar technique that you'll use for years to come.

Use the X's on this tab to show you exactly where the snare hits lay throughout the course of the riff:

```
e|--------x-------x------------------x-------x------------|e
B|--------x-------x------------------x-------x------------|B
G|--------x-------x------------------x-------x------------|G
D|--------x-------x------------------x-------x------------|D
A|--------x-------x---------0-0--x---2-2--x---------------|A
E|--0-0--x---0-0-x-3-------------x--------x---3-----------|E
```

29

*Always keep your pick above the string you're going to play next - This will help you do the quick move to play the third fret with your first finger after the clap/snare hit.

* Sit up straight & remember proper left and right hand technique.

CHAPTER 6

COME AS YOU ARE

Come As You Are

"Come As You Are" was Nirvana's second single off their album Nevermind, released in 1991. This was a notable time in music history when the Seattle grunge scene overthrew a pop dance style and "hair metal" that dominated the charts through the 80's. Kurt Cobain used an Electro Harmonix "Small Clone" guitar effects pedal on this riff which provides what is called a "chorus" effect. Also, Kurt's guitar was tuned down 1 full step lower than standard tuning.

Although "Come As You Are" didn't get as much recognition as "Smells Like Teen Spirit", its recognizable sound and simple fingering make it the perfect step up where I can introduce to you a good song with some new techniques.

Getting Ready

1. Look up "Come as you are - Nirvana" on the internet and have a listen.
2. Become familiar enough with the riff so you can hum along in real time.

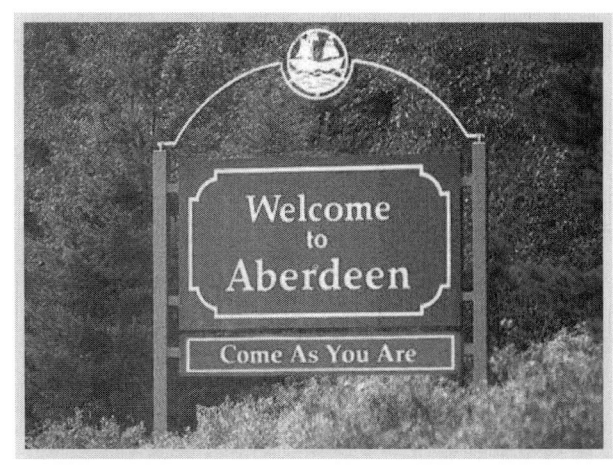

To honour Cobain, his hometown in Washington put up a sign that says "Welcome to Aberdeen - Come As You Are"

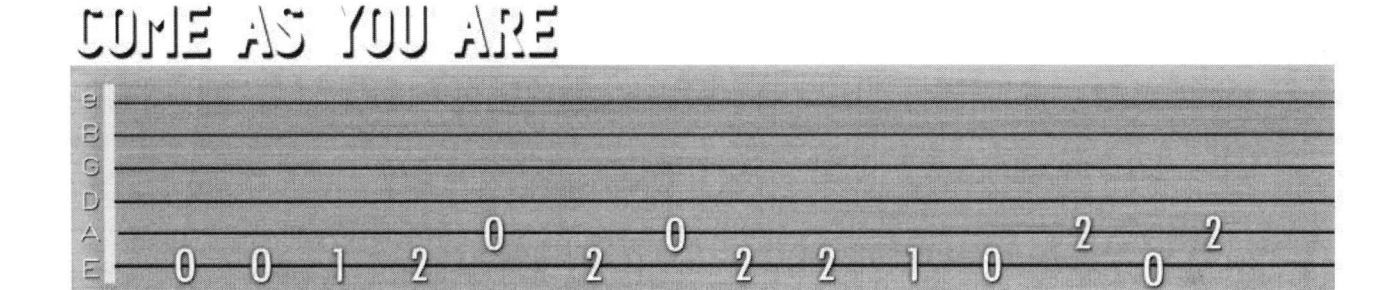

COME AS YOU ARE

```
e|------------------------------------------------|
B|------------------------------------------------|
G|------------------------------------------------|
D|------------------------------------------------|
A|--------------0-------0------------------2----2-|
E|--0--0--1--2-----2-------2--2--1--0---0-----0---|
```

Tips For This Riff & New Techniques:

To form a more complex tone, allow the notes to sound together.
- Every time you play the second fret, keep your finger down so that note sustains
- Every time you play an open string, let it ring/sustain

We're also going to incorporate alternate picking to this same area.
- Every note you play on the E string is a downstroke
- Every note you play on the A string is an up stroke.

And don't forget - use your stability points so you can play more accurately, leaving the ringing notes untouched.

CHAPTER 7

BORN UNDER A BAD SIGN

Born Under A Bad Sign

Albert king is a blues guitarist that became popular in the 60's. It became the first release and title track off the album, released in 1967. King recorded this song on his iconic "Gibson Flying-V". King played this right handed guitar left handed but the guitar remained strung for a right handed guitarist giving him a very unique approach to bending strings.

His sound remains legendary and was the influence of guitarists such as Stevie Ray Vaughan and Jimi Hendrix. Although King fronts the song in the recording, the words and music were actually written by the record labels rhythm and blues singer, William Bell and bandleader, Booker T. Jones (of Booker T. & the M.G.'s). For the blues, nothing beats a great guitar plugged straight into a loud and dirty tube amplifier. We're going to have fun with this one.

This riff uses 3 strings now using only your 1st and 3rd fingers.

Getting Ready

1. Look-up "Born Under A Bad Sign" and have a listen.
2. Become familiar enough with the riff so you can hum along in real time.

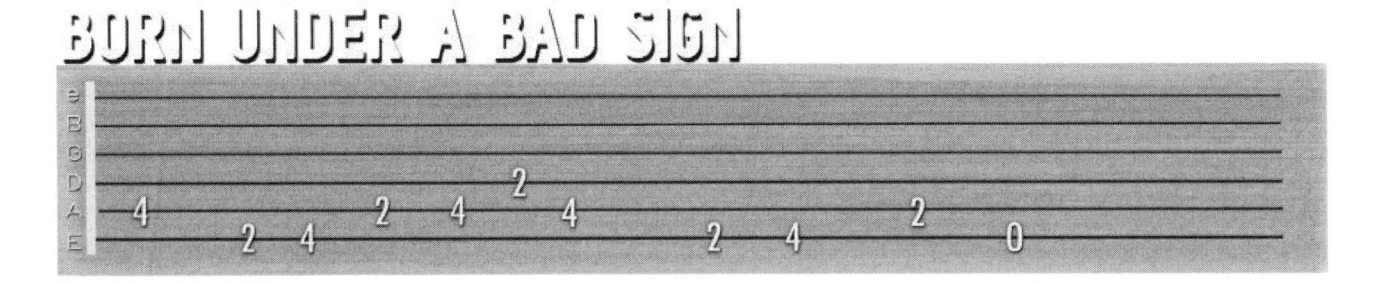

BORN UNDER A BAD SIGN

"Born Under A Bad Sign" - has a very cool call and response sound. Your fingering is based completely on the 2nd and 4th fret. It lines up well with using only your 1st and 3rd fingers. This is the first riff so far that is across 3 strings!

* Sit up straight & remember proper technique

* Try to feel the rhythm through your body and it will transfer through the guitar.

THE BLUES IS EASY TO PLAY, BUT HARD TO FEEL
— JIMI HENDRIX

IF YOU'VE GOT A BURNING DESIRE TO PLAY THE ELECTRIC BLUES, GET ACCESS TO

BLUES GUITAR STAR

THE BRAND NEW VIDEO SERIES FROM CAMPFIRE GUITAR STAR

Learn all the rhythm, improv and essential blues concepts that will have you playing stinging licks and stompy rhythms.

WWW.CAMPFIREGUITARSTAR.COM/BLUES

CHAPTER 8

HEY JOE

Hey Joe

Jimi Hendrix's rendition of "Hey Joe" is so good, it's hard to think of any other version. Despite its initial copyright in 1962 by Billy Roberts (a California folk singer) the original songwriter seems to be up for debate. Hendrix, with his signature style, used "Hey Joe" to introduce his band "The Jimi Hendrix Experience" to the world. Hendrix was a left handed player (Hey! Like Albert King & Kurt Cobain!). He played a right handed Fender Stratocaster but strung it upside down. Apparently, it was difficult to find left handed guitars in those days...

Before he was famous, he was "Jimmy James" - a working session guitarist that played behind many other very recognized musicians. Hendrix's mainstream career lasted only 4 years up to his death at the age of 27. He is known as one of the greatest guitar players that ever lived.

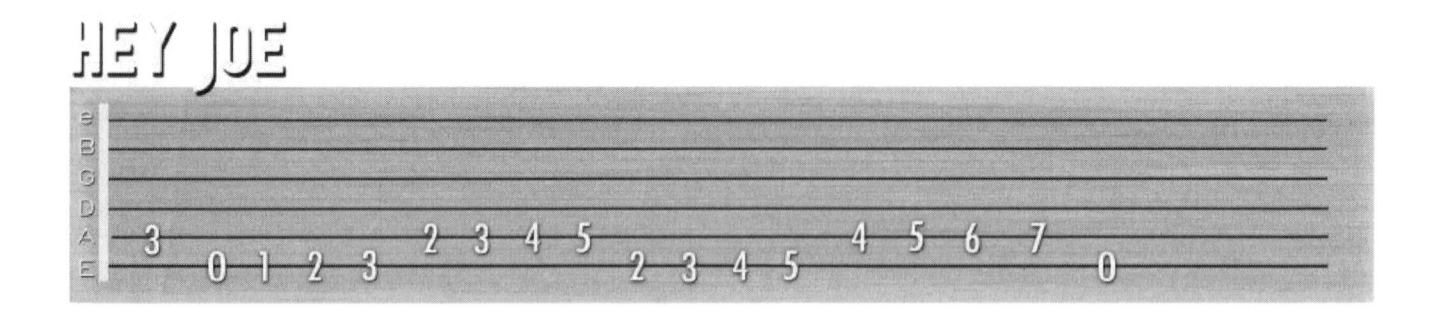

HEY JOE

```
e|---------------------------------------------------------------|
B|---------------------------------------------------------------|
G|---------------------------------------------------------------|
D|---------------------------------------------------------------|
A|--3-------------2-3-4-5-------------------4-5-6-7--------------|
E|------0-1-2-3-----------2-3-4-5--------------------0-----------|
```

This heavy, ascending style riff happens a few times throughout the song and shares a lot of similarities with your "warm-up scale". We're going to apply this "one-fret-at-a-time" movement to an actual, cool song. This will act as a great warm-up scale too!

If you have been practicing these riffs and your warm up scale, consider this your official warm-up scale graduation!

*By the way, we're using what in musical terms we would refer to as "chromatic techniques". Chromatic movements on the guitar are best described as one-fret-at-a-time movements.

Tips To Play This Riff

- Start on your third finger for that first note - the 3rd fret of the A string.
- Incorporate the alternate picking technique right from the beginning - When you switch strings it will always start on an upstroke for this riff.
- Make sure you're using all 4 fingers!

DISCOVERING YOUR NATURAL MOTIVATION - GET A GREAT PRACTICE ROUTINE

Just like many things in life, learning the guitar takes a bit of work. After some work comes a great satisfaction in learning new skills and putting them to use. There have been many studies that show how good learning and playing music is for us, and the best part, it's fun! Maybe one day there will be a 'guitar pill' and they will have the Slash pill and the Kirk Hammet pill and more. But until then…

We have to spend time on the guitar between lessons whether you're learning from a teacher 1-on-1 or from videos. Maybe you're wondering 'how often should I practice?' or 'how long do I practice for?' or have you ever wondered 'WHAT do I practice?'.

So whether you're following one of my online video lesson series, have a lesson with me 1-on-1 on Skype or in-person, maybe you've heard me share this philosophy:

"You only have to practice for 5 minutes a day"

I'll tell you how it works...

So what you need to do is find those pockets in your day - those 5, 10, 15, or 20 min time zones - before work, after work, before dinner, between meetings, before bed etc etc... the 'inbetween doing stuff' areas of your day. We all have them! My student who has 5 kids and 3 jobs still finds time to practice! So hold your excuses! When guitar becomes a priority in your life, you'll easily find this pockets in your day.

So when you arrive at the "in-between doing stuff" time-zone in your day, what you're going to say to yourself is this:

"I'm only going to play guitar for 5 min"

The trick here is just sitting down and putting a guitar in your lap. If you're on a real tight schedule, you're going to set a timer or at least watch the clock. At the end of the 5 minutes, here's what you're going to ask yourself:

"Do I have to go right now? Or can I play for a bit longer?"

This is up to your discretion. Playing the guitar and making time for it is THE MOST IMPORTANT THING. Often getting started is the hardest part. Don't feel guilty if you only practice for 5 minutes. Consider it a level of persistency that you're practicing. Small goals are good and they increase confidence.

Ok so good work! If you implement this simple 2 question process, you'll be playing guitar on a regular basis, daily in fact! Now, we gotta figure out how to squeeze every last drop out of these practice sessions so that we're using every minute effectively.

Here is a standard format for a solid practice session:

1. Warm-Up With A Metronome

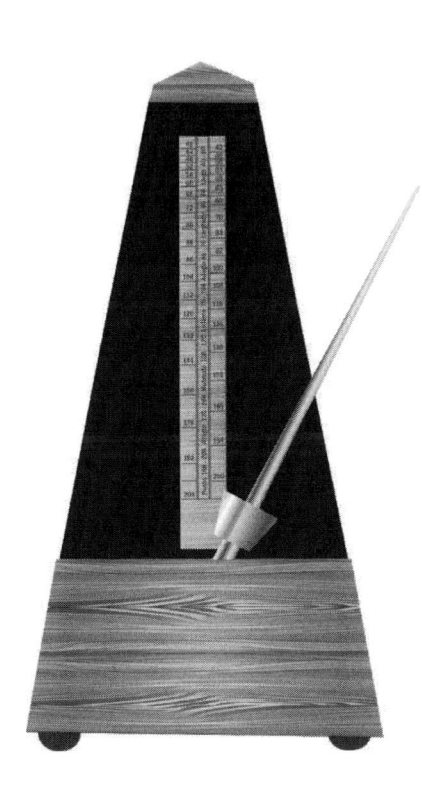

You can google search a metronome, get them on your smartphone, and of course get them from a music store.

Yup, we're "TAKING OUR FINGERS TO THE GYM!" Stronger, better, faster! This is what we're going to get by logging in time with the metronome.

I would suggest an E or A minor pentatonic scale or simply your warm-up scale to develop your accuracy, rhythm, technique and speed.

You need to really lock those notes on each click of the metronome. Excuse me for getting all 'jedi' on you, but - *"you must be **one** with the click."*

2. Play A Song That You Know

Maybe you don't know many songs, but pick a song that you're the most confident with and play that to warm-up even further.

3. Trouble Areas

Ok, we're warmed up, did a little working out and now we have to do some perfection of some guitar-isms!

You know those sections of a riff or a song or a lick that are causing some problems? That one chord change that you stumble over, EVERY TIME? Yup. THAT'S the part you want to focus on.

Many of my students don't recognize these sections their struggling with. So really perk up your ears and peel your eyes for those trouble areas. We've all had that one chord change that's just a pain. So let's take those 2 chords, whatever they may be and play it over, and over, and over and over and 1 time extra for good luck. Repetition is the only way! Although, we're talking about honing in on a very small area and repeating a very small section of a song.

Prime Example

For me personally, lately I've been learning this crazy Big Wreck solo from the song "A Million Days". YouTube the song and check it the solo. It's absolutely nutty!

I'll work on a lick over and over that is LITERALLY 0.5 OF A SECOND LONG from the track. I will put that to a metronome and repeat and repeat and slowly speed it up sometimes only increasing the speed by 1 bpm.

Often, the best way to learn something difficult is to break it down into smaller chunks. This will be a great thing to consider when you want to get to that next level of guitar playing.

4. See If You Can Introduce Something New

Keeping things fresh and learning songs that excite you is key. This is the 'natural motivation' that will keep the juices flowing and keep you moving forward.

If it's simply a chord you haven't played before, or a tabbed out riff, or a new song, this is the kinda stuff I want you to be hunting down!

Simply from here you can track down the new "trouble parts" and go back to step #3.

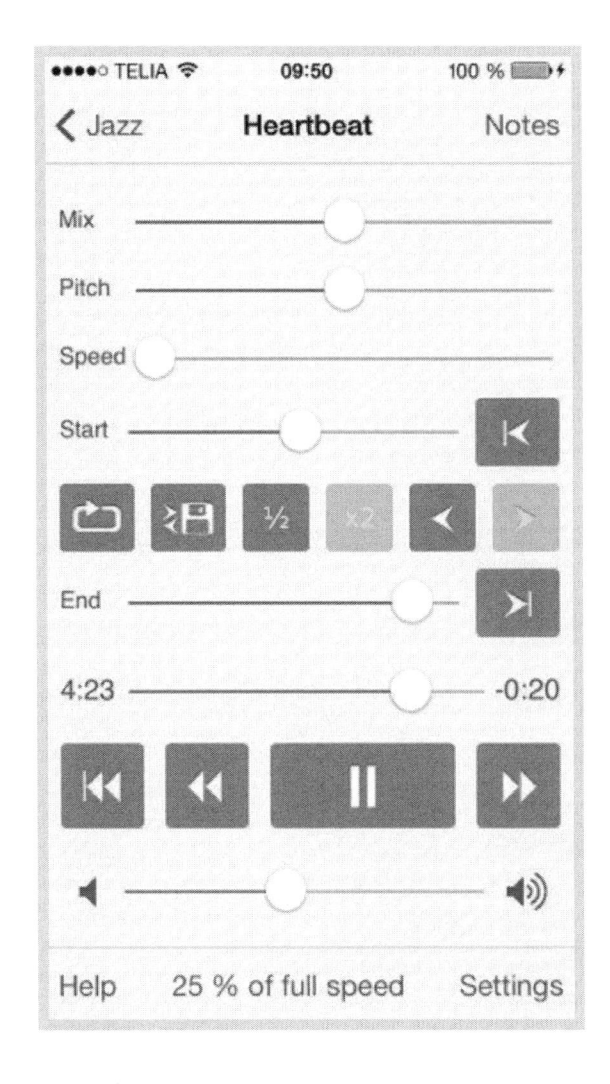

5. Keep track!

Keeping a log-book of your progression is a great way to remind you what you need to practice and will also keep track of your speeds with a metronome.

Another method of practicing is using programs like the "Amazing Slow Downer" by ronimusic.com. I can honestly say I've experienced a ton of value from using this program and so have many of my 1-on-1 students.

In Conclusion

Great guitarists have some kind of knack for details. The small details are the lead determining factor that will separate a beginner from a pro. Now of course there are a lot of small details, but if you just repeat step #3 on these trouble areas, you can work through your own small details and start being a better player right away.

And remember, you can trick yourself into practicing more often by saying **"I'm just going to play guitar for 5 minutes".** Then at the end of 5 minutes, either take off and feel proud that you made it a priority in your busy day, or you might find the 5 minute priority inspires you to play a little bit longer.

Here to help you play better and of course, keep on rippin it up!

MODULE 3

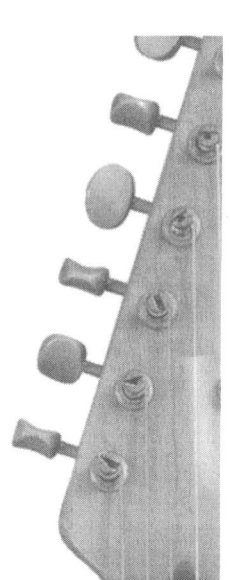

MUST KNOW SCALES

CHAPTER 9

THE MAJOR SCALE & SCALE CHARTS

The Major Scale & Scale Charts

Here's a jam packed lesson for you! One of our teachers here at Campfire Guitar Star, Mike B, refers to this as "Lesson-ception" in reference to the movie "Inception". In the movie, the characters experience "dreams inside of dreams" where new ideas can be formed. In "lesson-ception", there are "lessons inside of lessons", where new guitar concepts and a deeper understanding of the guitar are formed! So let's get started!

You probably know the major scale already! It's something very recognizable. You'll hear the "Sound of Music" tones as you play through the scale - "Do, Re, Mi, Fa, Sol, La, Ti, Do". It has a positive, happy sound as opposed to the darker and moodier sound of a minor scale. Another thing about the major scale is it is known as "Ionian". The name is from a series of 7 very important musical scales called "Modes". The major scale (aka "Ionian") is the first of the 7 modes. The next 6 modes, in order are: Dorian, Phrygian, Lydian, Mixolydian, Aeolian, and

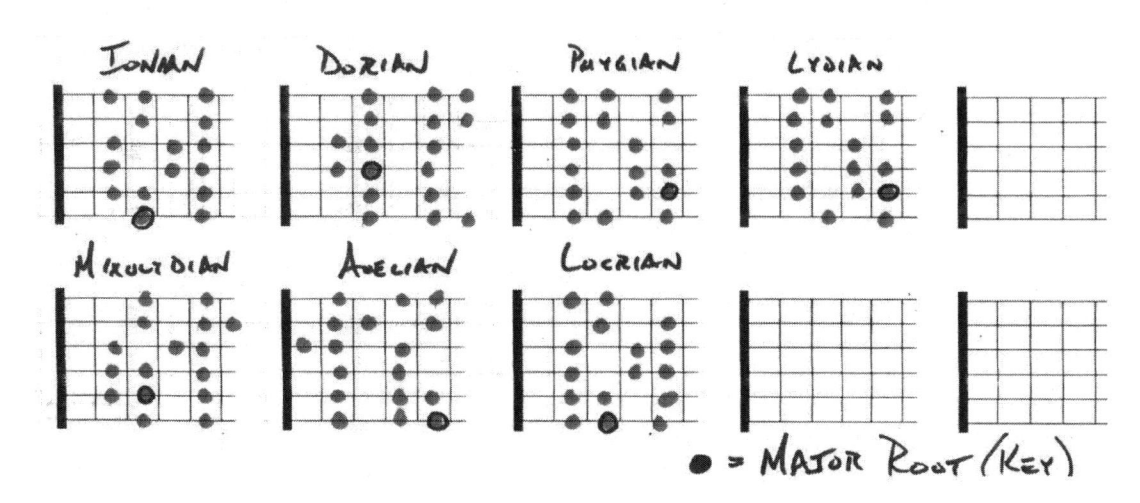

● = MAJOR ROOT (KEY)

Locrian. After going through this chapter and when you fully understand how to read scale charts, I encourage you to learn all 7 modes!

All the modes are fantastic finger exercises and the foundation for understanding how music works. They are also the building blocks of many famous solos, riffs and licks…. So if you like that kind of thing, then you're in for a treat! And some hard work :)

Reading A Scale Chart With The G Major Scale

*Remember when we were learning to read tab? The numbers were in reference to the frets you play… things change a bit now with scale charts.

Scale charts have numbers that represent your fingering - not which fret to use. Do not fear! Scale charts will show you which frets to place your fingers on. Scale charts (and chord charts) show you a diagram as if you were looking right down on top of the fret board. Take a look at the pictures - Can you see how the note on the fretboard diagram is translated to the guitar?

Note: Sometimes scale diagrams are vertical like in the example we have here, but they can also be represented horizontally - similar to tab. Just remember that how we read scale and chord charts is very different from how we read tab.

*Because we can start scales on any fret, it's often unnecessary to have a diagram of the entire fretboard. You will know what scale you are playing from your root note!

Two ways to discover the correct fret, or starting point, on a scale chart:

G Major Scale

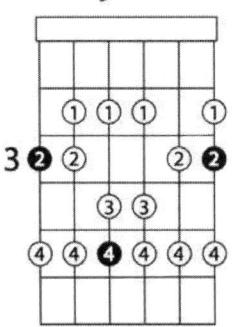

1. The "Nut", or block at the end of the fretboard, will give you a visual representation of where you are. (In case you don't know what the nut is - find the diagram of the parts of the guitar found inside this book.)
2. A number indicating the fret beside the chart will tell you exactly where to start your first note.

Starting with your second finger on the third fret, go through the G major scale one note at a time. When you get to the end, do the same thing in reverse.

The Big Secret To Playing ANY Scale

Complete all the notes on one string before moving to the next string. Start with your lowest note on the low E string, play the next note in the sequence to complete all the notes of the scale on the E string before you move on to the A string.

So in this example, you would play the 3rd fret of the E string (with your 2nd finger) and then play the 5th fret of the E string (with your pinky finger/4th finger). Then you would move to the 2nd fret of the A string with your first finger and do all 3 notes on the A string before moving to the D string and so on. Often scales have at least 2 notes per string. In the case of the G Major Scale that I'm showing you here, there are 2-3 notes per string. So just remember that you need to complete ALL the notes on each string before you move onto the next string.

Lastly, just like your warm up scale, you want to prioritize these 3 things, in this order:

#1. Clear Notes   **#2 Consistency**   **#3 Speed**

A great way to practice your scales is with a metronome! You can just search "online metronome" in your favorite search engine or there are many free apps like "Pro Metronome" in the Apple App Store. This tool will help you especially with #2 consistency (so you can improve your rhythm) and #3 Speed (you can keep track of how fast you can play it).

The scales we will learn next are actually EASIER than the major scale so stay tuned.

CHAPTER 10

POWER CHORDS & INTERVALS
SIMPLE & POWERFUL ROCK GUITAR TECHNIQUES

Power Chords & "Intervals"

Back to the fun stuff! The first chord we're going to learn is the power chord. It's only 2 notes, it's extremely versatile, and it sounds...well... powerful!

With the G major scale fresh in mind, let me introduce to you the G5, or the "G power chord". Remember the "Lesson-ception" concept? Here's another lesson we can draw from that major scale.

A G5 chord consists of 2 notes - Your G (root note) combined with the 5th note of the major scale. It's really that simple. This is a great way to understand what an "interval" is. Using your major scale, you can start to understand what major 3rds, perfect 4ths, perfect 5ths are and more. They're just notes from the major scale that are associated or related to your first note. An interval!

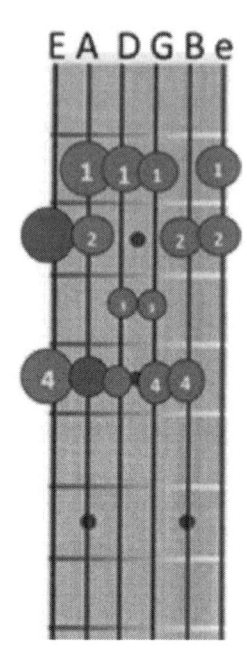

To play a power chord - let's reference the scale chart here. Play your G note with your first finger. Then, 2 frets up and one string over, you'll find the 5th note of the scale or "the 5th" with your third finger. When you play these 2 notes at the same time, you get a "power chord". This is the most common way to play a power chord, but there are a few different fingerings for power chords. So let's talk about the next most common power chord shape.

*If you're wondering about the orange marker and your 4th (or pinky) finger isn't on it yet, try it out!

More Lesson-Ception - "The Octave" In Power Chords, Drawn Out From Your Major Scale

This orange mark is the "octave", or eighth note of the scale (take a look at that word - it's got "oct" meaning 8). It's the same note as the first note of the major scale, just sounding higher up! This interval is called a "perfect octave".

When you add it to your power chord, notice how it sounds just tiny bit thicker, or just subtly more 'powerful'. This string you're fretting with your pinky finger is also a G, so we're actually **not** adding a new note. Just stacking an additional note to fill it out a bit more.

Here Are 4 Different Finger Placements Of Power Chords That You Can Use For Powerful Results!

Have some fun with these shapes and see if you can switch 2 or 3 power chords together and make something sound musical. Try moving this exact same power chord shape over one string to the A-string. You can play this power chord shape on any fret of the guitar, starting on the E-string or the A-string!

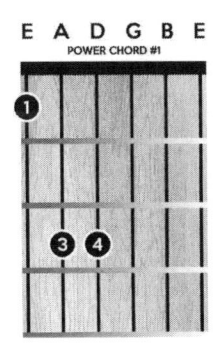

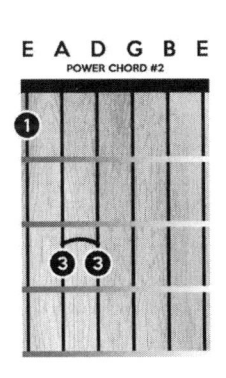

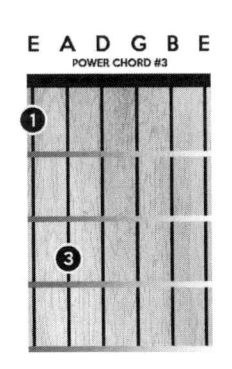

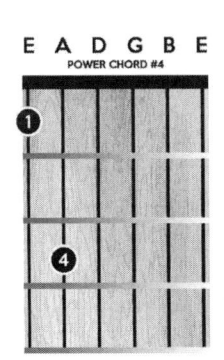

Another Way To Look At It:
Here are these different power chords tabbed out

*Note: these might make more sense after the "Advanced tab" section (chapter 14)

```
G5 (G power chord)        G5 (G power chord)
Version #1 and #2         Version #3 and #4

e|x|                      e|x|
B|x|                      B|x|
G|x|                      G|x|
D|5|                      D|x|
A|5|                      A|5|
E|3|                      E|3|
```

Powerful Tips For Powerful Chords:

- Reference the last chapter on scale charts to read these chords.
- These are visual representations of what power chords look like. It's like your looking right down on top of the fret board. We will discuss more about chord charts in later chapters.
- The numbers are referencing which fingers you can use.
- Power chord #2 references the use of a "barre" with your 3rd finger - this is playing 2 notes at the same time with 1 finger (You can press on 2 strings using your 3rd finger).
- I personally use all of these shapes and I would recommend getting used to all of them and figuring out which ones work the best for the application at hand.
- Remember to play **only** the notes in the chord and not random open strings.
- Plow your pick through all the notes simultaneously - make these chords sound full and powerful!
- With all of this exciting new knowledge, it can be easy to forget some things. If you haven't already, go back and review the first couple of chapters on proper technique before moving on.

CHAPTER 11

PENTATONIC SCALES
- MUST KNOW SCALES -

Pentatonic Scales

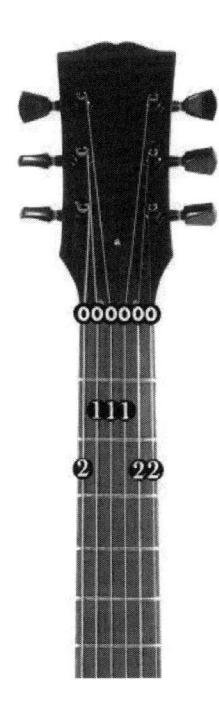

Now that you're starting to get familiar with terms like "fifths" and "octaves", we're about to open the door to "Pentatonic Scales". They are like normal scales with less notes!

Typically, scales have 7 notes. Pentatonic scales have 5 notes. That's what makes Pentatonic scales special!

Penta = 5 Tonic = Tone

Pentatonic scales (especially minor pentatonics) are the framework for some of the most famous Rock, and Blues songs. That riff you thought sounded so powerful, that solo you can't get out of your head, good chance it's based on a pentatonic scale!

Here on the left we have an E Minor Pentatonic Scale. If you need a refresher on how to play scale charts, check out the lesson on the major scale.

Now take a look at the A minor pentatonic scale here on the right of page 51. The Emi and

Ami pentatonic scales, although they feel a lot different, are exactly the same scale, just played in a different key using and therefore, using different fingers. In the Emi scale, all of your open strings can be played, in the Ami scale, your first finger is playing all the notes on the 5th fret taking the place of the nut.

Practicing These New Scales

Aside from practicing these over and over like crazy (which I recommend) with proper technique, a metronome and developing the 3 pillars of scales: Clean notes, consistency and speed - we can also use the internet as a great tool.

Searching for "backing tracks" on the internet, or jamming along in the same key as your favorite songs, is one of the best ways to start putting your pentatonic scales to use.

You can try searching "Emi backing track" or "Ami backing track" or "Emi blues rhythm track" etc on YouTube and put your new knowledge to work! You'll probably notice that the notes you're playing on the guitar sound "right" against the backing track! Welcome to the land of improv!

Blues Scales

BLUES SCALES

E Blues Scale

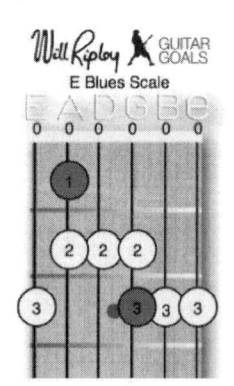

*Note: The blues scale has only 1 added note to the minor pentatonic scale (the one colored blue) It's often referred to as "The blue note" It's technical term is the b5 (flat 5)

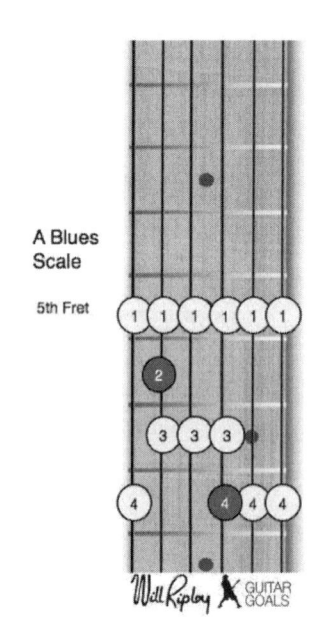

A Blues Scale
5th Fret

By now, we're getting to know the sounds of different scales. With the "Blues scale", shown in the chart here, the sound is in the name. Adding 1 more note to each octave of the pentatonic scale will make it perfect for a moodier, bluesy sound. Because the scale goes through 2 octaves, it may feel and seem like we're adding 2 new notes to the pentatonic scale, but trust me - it's just 1 extra note!

LET PEOPLE KNOW WHO YOU ARE AND WHAT YOU DO!

Let Everyone Know You're A **"Campfire Guitar Star"**

Get t-shirts and more at
WWW.CAMPFIREGUITARSTAR.COM/MERCH

MODULE 4

POWER CHORD ROCK SONGS

CHAPTER 12

CONFUSED BY TAB?
DISCOVER THE SECRETS OF TABLATURE

Advanced Tab

If you are comfortable reading tab so far, this will be nice and straight forward. Take a look at this screenshot from the video. When you have 2 notes in-line or right on top of one another in tab, they are simply played at the same time. This example "0" and "2", you'll see they are written one on top of the next and not one after another.

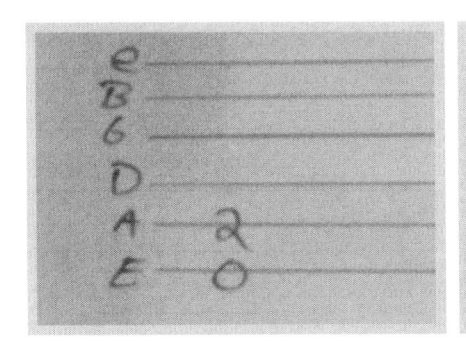

With your first finger on the second fret of the A string, play these two notes together by strumming down on the 2 strings simultaneously.

Generally tab doesn't tell you which fingers to use, but as you progress, you'll find the best ways of using your fingers and it will become more apparent which fingers should be used when you're working your way through tablature.

You can see another example on page 55.

Again, looking at the tab on the left, play the second fret of the A string with your first finger and the 4th fret of the D string with your third finger.

*"0" written in tab will always indicate playing the string open.

*Remember, the difference between scale charts and tab - When reading tab, the numbers reference what frets to play. When reading chord charts, the numbers (if written on the strings) indicate your fingering.

The songs we have been learning up to this point are essentially bass lines on the guitar. The next set of songs will step up your playing to incorporate new techniques like 2 notes at a time and power chords.

Must Know "Open Power Chords" Tabbed Out:

Open power chords use the exact same formula as what I've been teaching - just utilizing open strings. These are the types of chords that a band like AC/DC loves. Actually, try going E5, D5 D5 D5, A5 A5 A5 and you have the opening chords to "Back in Black"!

```
E5 (E power chord)      A5 (A power chord)      D5 (D power chord)
e|x|                    e|x|                    e|x|
B|x|                    B|x|                    B|3 (or just x)|
G|x|                    G|2|                    G|2|
D|2|                    D|2|                    D|0|
A|2|                    A|0|                    A|x|
E|0|                    E|x|                    E|x|
```

GUITAR TABLATURE LEGEND

CHAPTER 13

IRON MAN

"Iron Man" was released with little mainstream attention on Black Sabbath's 2nd studio album "Paranoid" in 1970. It had a cult following and grew in success over the years eventually earning a spot on Rolling Stone magazines "500 Greatest Songs of All Time" and even a Grammy for "Best Metal Performance" in 2000. The only thing this song has in common with the Iron Man movies and comics is its title. The song tells the tale of a man who travels into the future and witnesses the apocalypse. Upon his return to the present to warn humanity, he is turned to steel by a magnetic field and ends up becoming the cause of the destruction he had witnessed.

*This song will introduce power chords in a challenging yet straightforward way. Make sure you're in tune, you're sitting straight are warmed up.

The power chord is always the same formula; take some breaks & stretch. We're taking our fingers to the gym!

IRON MAN

```
e|-----------------------------------------------------------|
B|-----------------------------------------------------------|
G|-----------------------------------------------------------|
D|--4----7--7--9--9---12-11--12-11--12-11---7--7--9--9-------|
A|--2----5--5--7--7---10--9--10--9--10--9---5--5--7--7-------|
E|-----------------------------------------------------------|
```

You can keep your power chord shape pressed down and even slide between the power chords like this example.

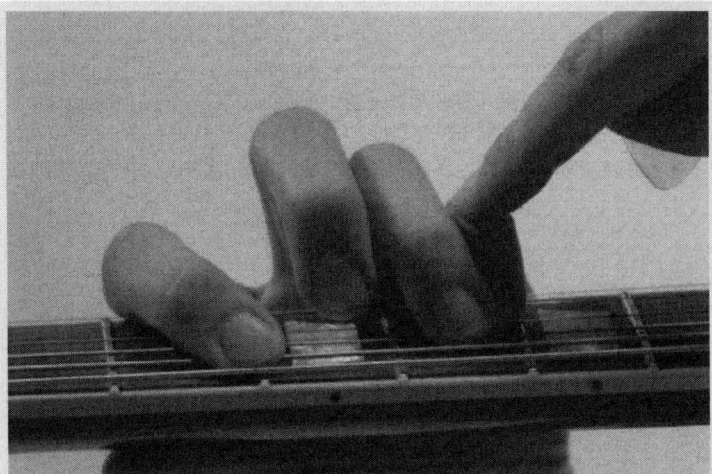

- Play your power chords with your first and third finger.
- When you're ready to take the next step, add the root note with your pinky finger for a fuller sounding power chord!
- Plow through the two strings with your right hand and use the D string (that you don't play) to stop the pick.
- If you find the last section of the riff to be too challenging, try using your first finger to go between the 10th and 9th fret. It's a good way to start working on the fast change and to eventually play a full power chord!

*Don't forget about the basic ground rules - listen to the song, get it in your head so you know what you're trying to achieve.

CHAPTER 14

21 GUNS

"21 Guns" was released in 2009 on Green Day's 8th studio album. The whole album had a very political feel and was described as a "rock opera". The title of the song references a military gun salute, and gives a response to those suffering in America.

This song is questionably easier than "Iron Man" and is a great way to start getting a handle on power chords.

21 GUNS

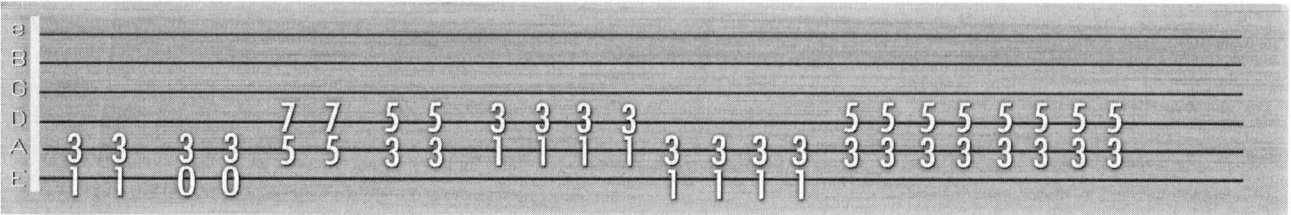

```
e|----------------------------------------------------------------|
B|----------------------------------------------------------------|
G|----------------------------------------------------------------|
D|------------7-7---5-5---3-3-3-3-------------5-5-5-5-5-5-5-5-----|
A|-3-3---3-3--5-5---3-3---1-1-1-1---3-3-3-3---3-3-3-3-3-3-3-3-----|
E|-1-1---0-0------------------------1-1-1-1-----------------------|
```

*In the frame shot progression on the left, you can see the first two chords of the song. Note that the second chord isn't a power chord.

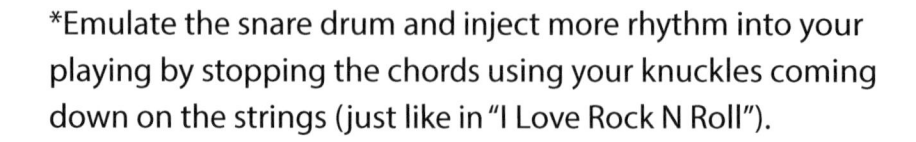

*Emulate the snare drum and inject more rhythm into your playing by stopping the chords using your knuckles coming down on the strings (just like in "I Love Rock N Roll").

*Your right hand should be playing all downstrokes. Remember to use the string below the ones you're playing as your pick stopper.

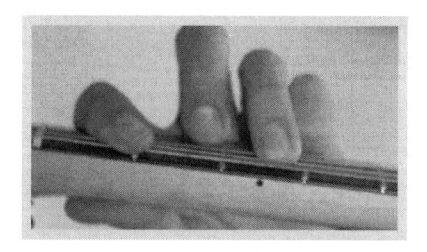

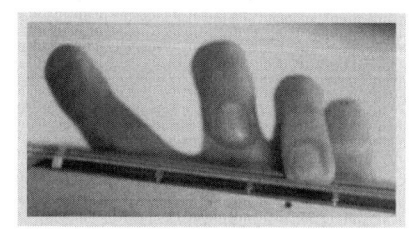

CHAPTER 15

ROCK GUITAR
TECHNIQUES USING POWER CHORDS

Palm Muting

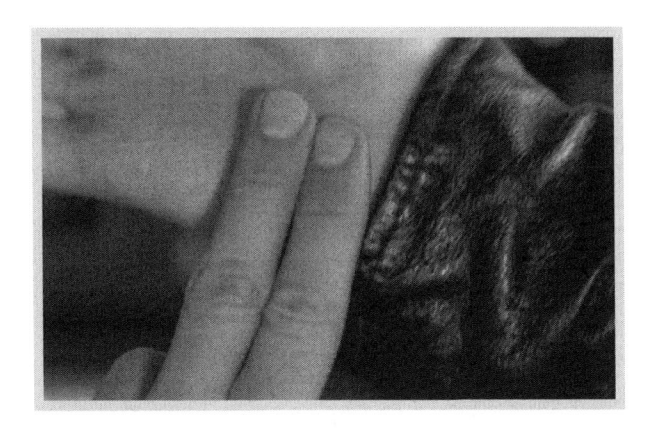

Palm muting is an awesome technique that every guitarist should get dialed in. It's that muffled, super rhythmic sound that creates some very iconic guitar sounds. Think about (or YouTube) the intro to "Barracuda" by Heart or the intro to "Welcome To The Jungle" by GnR. Yup, those guitarists are using palm muting in a big way to make those riffs sound amazing!

Muting the strings with your palm sounds straightforward, but there are some tricks you should know. If you have been practicing the right hand technique from the beginning, you'll already be in position. It's a very important guitar technique so here's the steps. Your thumb pillow is about to expand across your wrist and other sections of your hand.

1. With your right hand planted on the bridge, choose a power chord and strum down strokes.

2. While strumming, slowly move the base of your

palm up the strings towards the headstock and listen to how the sound changes.

3. When the sound becomes too muffled and you think you've gone too far, back off a bit to find that sweet spot.

- The area of your hand that you'll use to mute the strings varies slightly with different players.

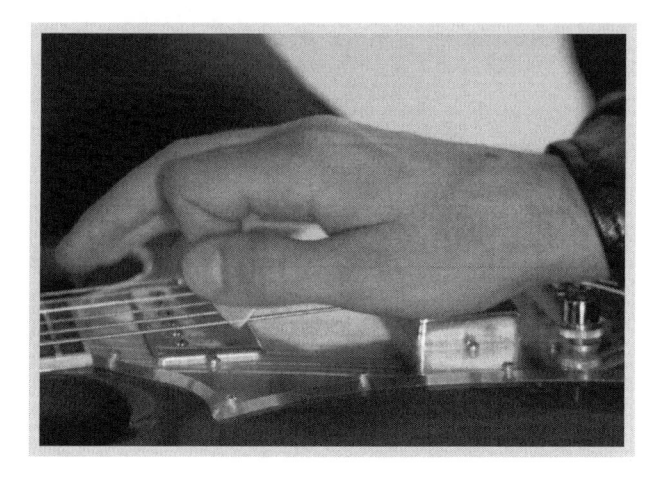

- Note that your palm muting technique changes when you use a guitar strap and stand up. When your guitar is lower on your body, you will use the right edge of your hand along side your pinky finger. Otherwise, the same rules apply - just find the sweet spot to mute the strings to get that cool muffled, rhythmic guitar sound!

CHAPTER 16

POWER CHORD GRADUATION
I LOVE ROCK N' ROLL

I Love Rock & Roll (pt.2)

Here comes your power chord graduation!

Reference the tab that you see in this chapter. Make sure you're using proper fingering (1st and 3rd) for your power chords. It will leave your second finger free and in a good position to get that third fret of the E string.

I LOVE ROCK N' ROLL

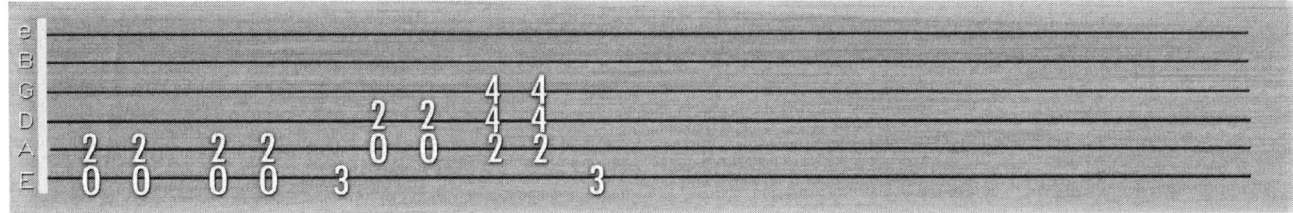

```
e|---------------------------------|
B|---------------------------------|
G|---------------------------------|
D|-------------2-2---4-4-----------|
A|-2-2---2-2---0-0---2-2-----------|
E|-0-0---0-0-3-------------3-------|
```

So, as mentioned, this is your power chord graduation. This is an opportunity to utilize and execute what you've learned so far up until now.

As you might remember, we learned "I Love Rock N' Roll" as a bassline/single note riff like this:

I LOVE ROCK N' ROLL

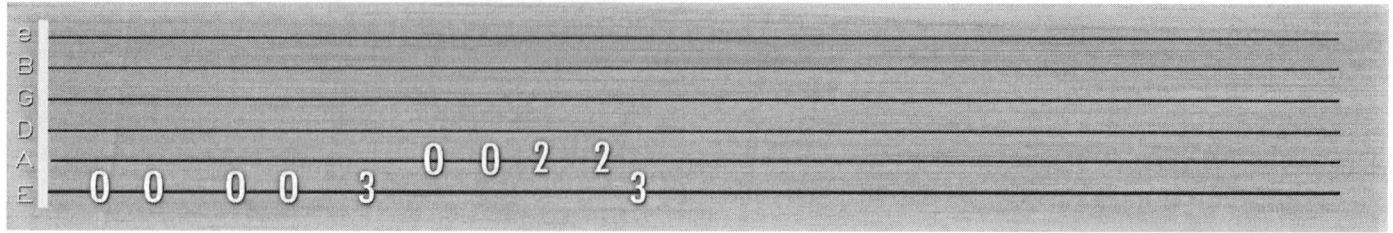

```
e|-----------------------------------------------|e
B|-----------------------------------------------|B
G|-----------------------------------------------|G
D|-----------------------------------------------|D
A|--0-0---0-0--3-----0--0--2--2----3-------------|A
E|--------------------------------3--------------|E
```

With this "power chord" version, we're going to extend the notes into full power chords which will get your riff a lot closer to the original recording.

This songs starts with an E5 chord, uses an A5 chord and a B5 chord. Remember, that's just like saying an "E power chord", an "A power chord" and a "B power chord".

These techniques and chords are all over rock music. A band like AC/DC comes to mind. Rage Against The Machine also used these exact chords and techniques on the chorus of "Bullet in the Head". They are truly universal, must-know guitar skills that can be used across a wide variety of music.

Remember to get those "claps" that mimic the snare drum throughout the riff. It'll really make this song sound great. After the clap, get the pick on top of the next string you're going to play so you're ready to go.

*Bend the low E string with your second finger when playing the 3rd fret to make the riff sound juicy! In the tab below you'll see "3b" to remind you.

Here's the tab to let you know where the snare hits happen (x)

```
e|-------x-------x---------------x-------x-------------|e
B|-------x-------x---------------x-------x-------------|B
G|-------x-------x----------2-2--x---4-4-x-------------|G
D|--2-2--x---2-2-x----------2-2--x---4-4-x-------------|D
A|--2-2--x---2-2-x----------0-0--x---2-2-x-------------|A
E|--0-0--x---0-0-x-3b------------x-------x-3b----------|E
```

63

GUITAR SOLO LIKE A BOSS

Who Doesn't Love A Good Guitar Solo?

Unlock The Techniques, Licks, Solos, Scales And Vocabulary To Play Classic Solos From Led Zeppelin To Van Halen To Nirvana With Campfire Guitar Star's Brand New Video Series: "Lead Guitar Star"

Discover More At
WWW.CAMPFIREGUITARSTAR.COM/LEAD

MODULE 5

MASTER GUITAR CHORDS

CHAPTER 17

CHORD CHARTS
LEARN TO PLAY ANY CHORD (START WITH THIS ONE)

Chordal Discovery: Everything You Need To Know About Reading Chords

Chord Charts and the Em Chord, Cadd9 and A Maj

Chords are a combination of notes that are played at the same time. Mixing notes creates harmonies for a more full and complex sound.

In this lesson we'll talk about 3 important chords and talk about all the strategies and techniques you'll want to know so you can play any chord. We will also talk about a technique called arpeggios and how to arpeggiate chords.

Here are 3 chord charts that represent the exact same chord, E minor. However, you'll notice that the diagrams are all slightly different. What are the only differences?

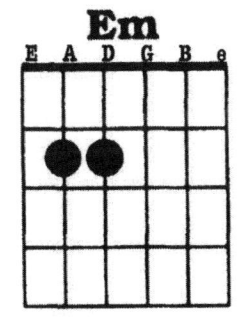

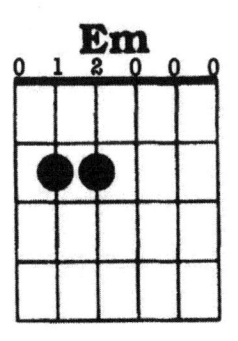

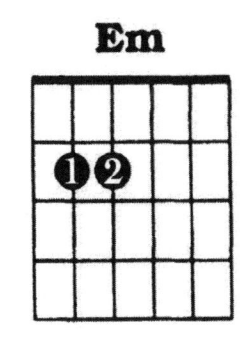

Sometimes you will see chords written with no indicated fingering. Sometimes the fingering is written across the top in place of the string names. On other chord charts, you'll see the numbers written right inside the dots.

Like we've talked about in previous chapters, chord diagrams are just a visual representation of the fret board. When you see the thick line on the top of the diagram, often that's in reference to the nut (a part near the headstock of the guitar). When you make that connection, it's often easy to see that a chord diagram is just like if you were to use a birds eye view, right down on top of the fret board.

Often times my students are able to make the connection between chords charts by just holding their guitars right next to the chord diagram because that's all it really is - a picture of the first few frets of the guitar!

So here's what an Emi chord looks like on the guitar. Can you make the connection between the chord diagram and the actual finger placement on the guitar?

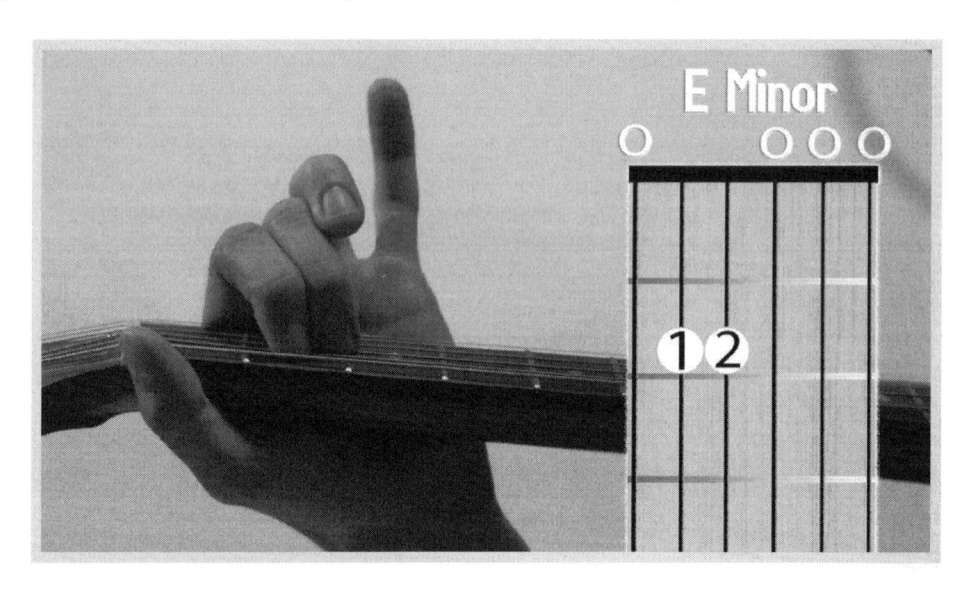

Next, let's get a bit more into it using all 4 fretting fingers and play this very important, common chord - the Cadd9 chord. It's basically just a C Major chord. However, it has an additional "color note" that's referred to as the "9". Therefore, the full name of the chord is C Major Add 9. Because that's a bit of a long name, us guitar players refer to it as just the Cadd9.

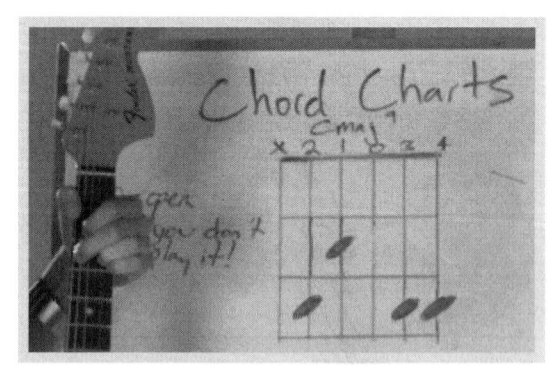

Can you see how the chord diagram and the placement of the guitar are related?

Here's another angle of the Cadd9 chord:

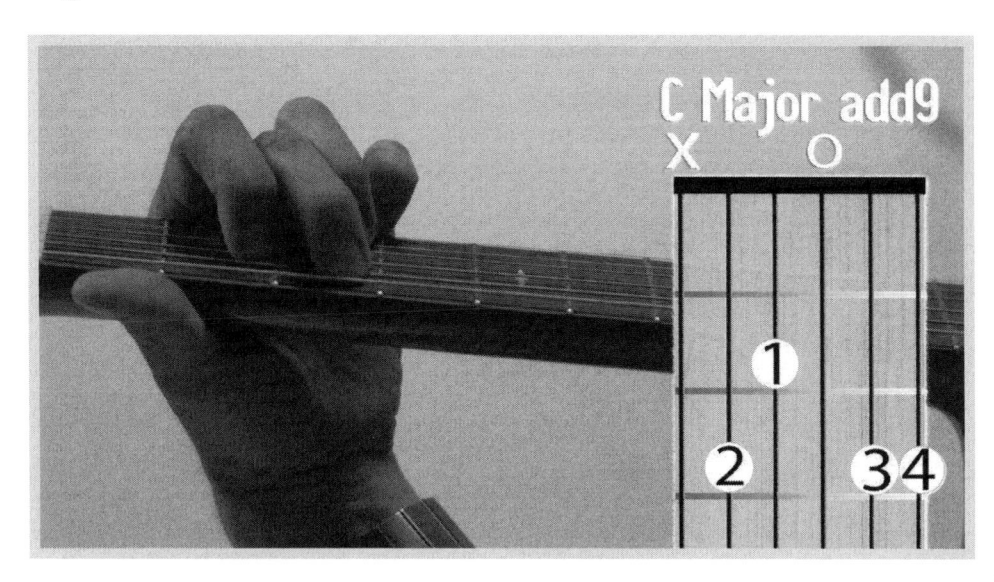

So the numbers are in reference to which fingers you use - you count 1,2,3,4 and generally this excludes your thumb. See the picture to see which finger is associated with which number.

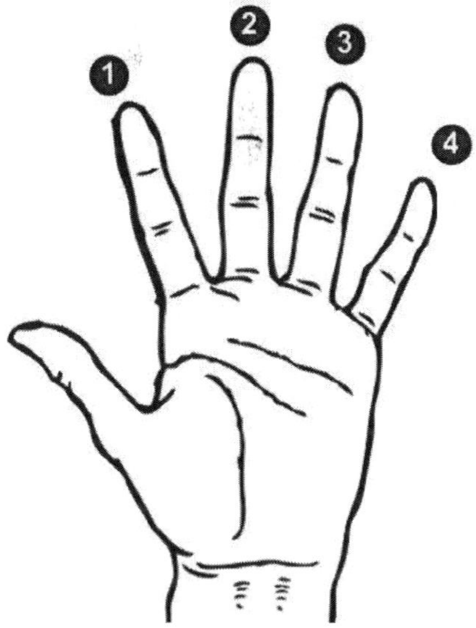

But maybe you're also noticing the "O" and and "X". These simply are showing you which strings to strum and which strings to avoid. I like to think of "O" as "open".

Next, let's talk about the only other thing that you'll run into on chord diagrams. Let me introduce you to the "barre". This is when we use 1 finger to cover multiple strings. It's like your finger forms a steel bar to support the notes. The A Major chord is a great example that we can use because this is also a very common, must-know chord.

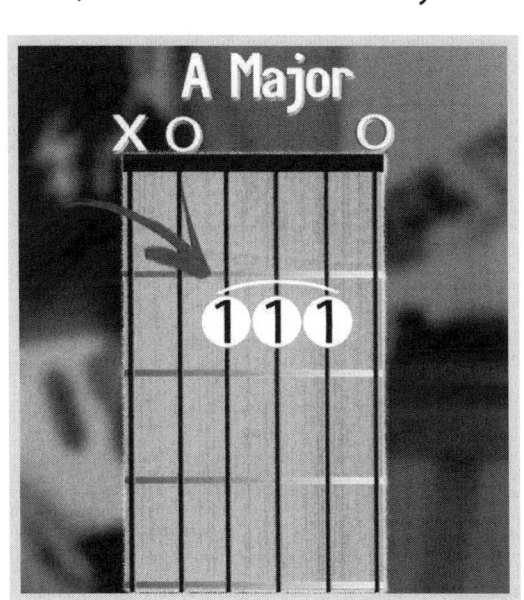

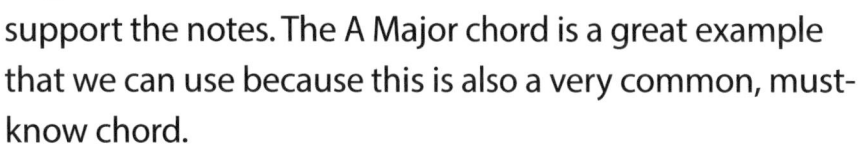

Now, I will say right away that you see a ton of different ways of playing an A Major chord. I really recommend you use this fingering I have laid out for you here. Why use 3 fingers when you can just use 1, right?

Look at this curved line above the notes on the A Major chord diagram. The line indicates a "barre" because it uses only 1 finger.

Getting your first finger to bend at the knuckle will really help to get this chord to sound clear.

Here's what the A Major chord looks like from your point of view. Can you see how the chord chart translates to the guitar?

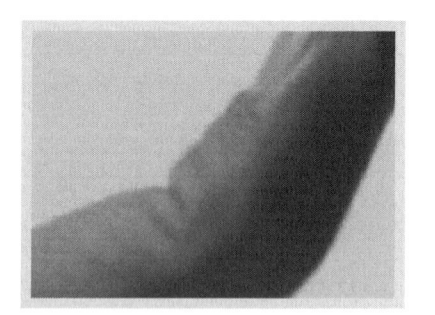

Chords On Other Places Of The Guitar

Of course, chords exist on other parts of the neck too. You'll know where to start the scale or chord because of some kind of numbering beside the diagram. It will always be clear what fret to start from. In the chords we're going to focus on now however, you'll only have to be concerned with the first 3 frets. That's where most of the magic happens on guitar anyways.

69

Tips To Play Chords

A common beginner mistake is accidentally muting strings that should be played in the chord. After finding your finger position, "arpeggiating" will help you uncover any problem notes if they exist. Playing one string at a time, you'll find the unintentionally muted or buzzy strings.
Another way of looking at arpeggiating is the word "articulating". It's like you articulate each note in the chord to be sure it's sounding clean and clear.

- *If you're having trouble, try putting your thumb on the back of the neck to help provide more of a squeezing position between your thumb and fingers. This will help you press down the strings harder. Check out this diagram. As you progress, you'll be able to take advantage of pro techniques when your thumb is NOT in this position. This might just be a crutch for you to get the finger muscles strengthened for now.*

- Double check that your fingers are as close up to the frets as possible.

- When getting chords to sound clear, your fingers need to be almost vertical off of the fretboard - not leaned over.

- On chord charts. "0" means open. You can also think of the letter "O" for "open". This means that you do want to play that string.

- "X" means you avoid that string or don't play that string.

- Consider every string that should be played and every string that should be muted.

CHAPTER 18

EASY CHORDS
FOR BEGINNERS - THE BEST CHORDS TO LEARN **FIRST**

The Best Chords To Learn First - All The Chords You Need To Know

In the last chapter, we learned about reading chord charts and we covered an E minor, Cadd9 and A major.

In this chapter we're going to continue this process of learning more, **must-know** chords. You can probably guess there are <u>a lot</u> of chords that you can play on the guitar. Knowing the chords that I'm about to show you will be the best start to playing many classic songs.

I want to show you the C major D major, E major, G major, A minor, and E Minor.

We're skipping over the really tough chords that honestly, a beginner guitar player doesn't need to worry about.

If you follow the chapters all the way through until the end, I will show you how to play every single major and minor chord, up to 3 different ways! But until then, let's focus on these important, basic chords.

Starting with a D chord, we will talk about some techniques that you should keep in mind for ALL your chords:

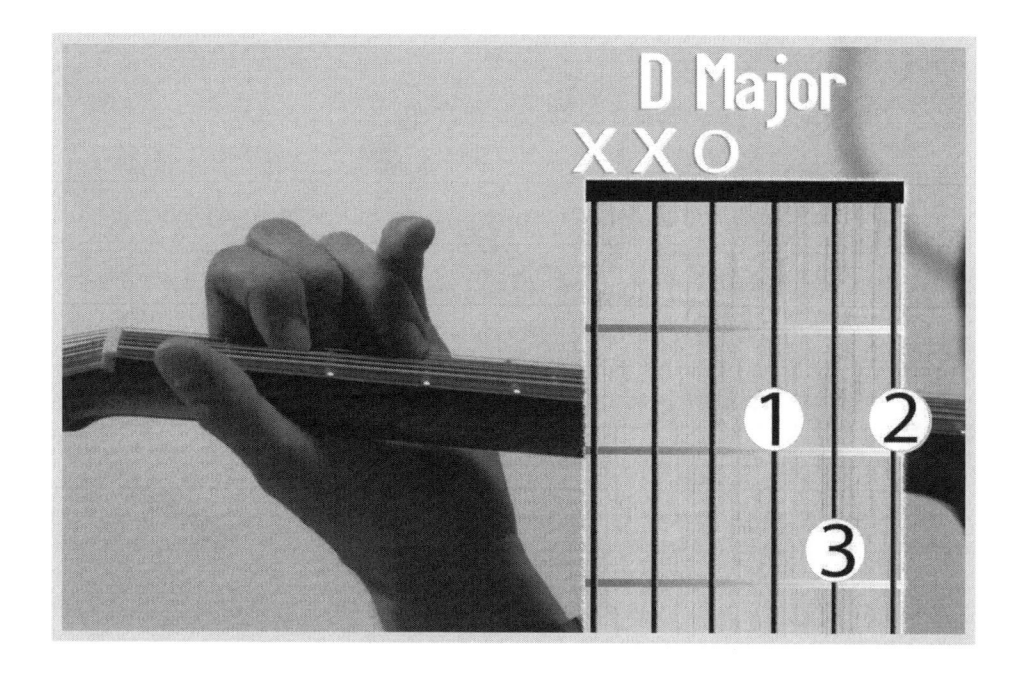

Take a look at these 2 pictures. One (on the left), you'll see my fingers laying down on top of the strings. This will remove the necessary pressure to get the chords sounding good. It will also mute a string or two... **not** what we want!

Get those fingers standing up straight. Allow all 3 fingers to fret properly and let the strings/notes ring out clearly like the picture on the right:

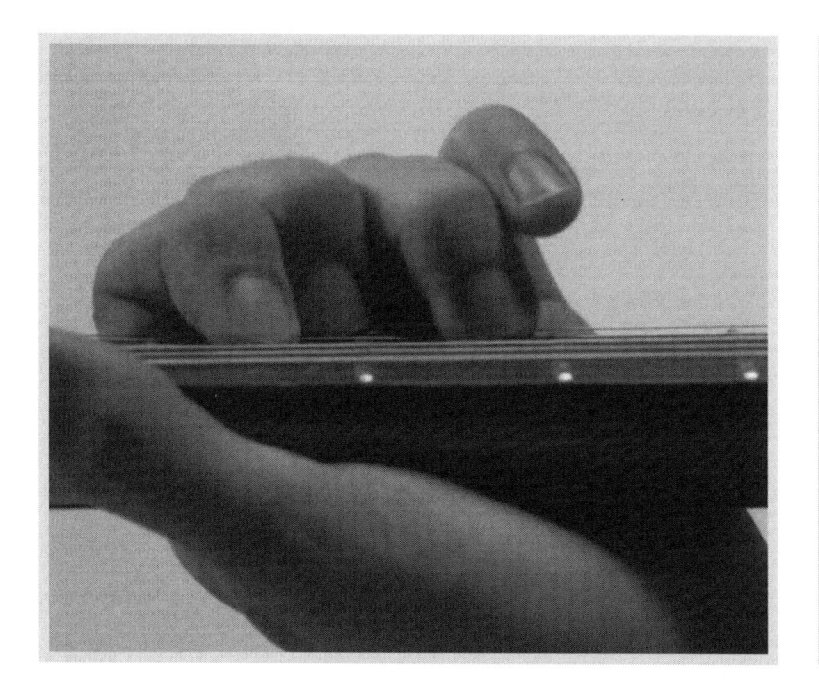

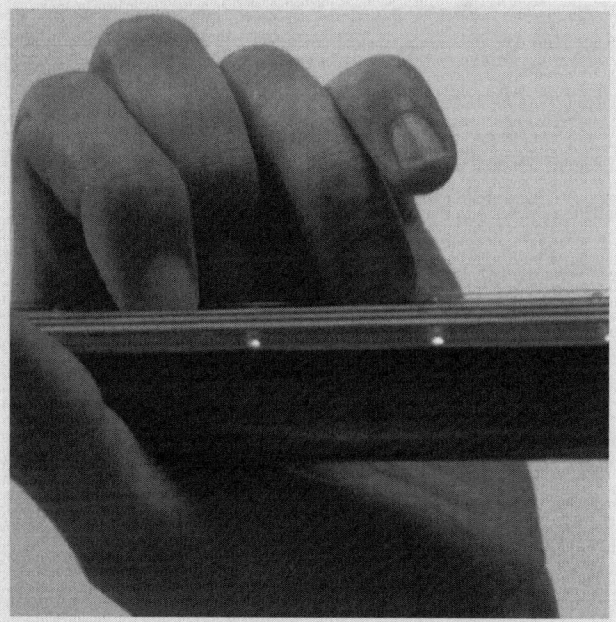

This is a great rule for what you want to do with ALL your chords.

G Major

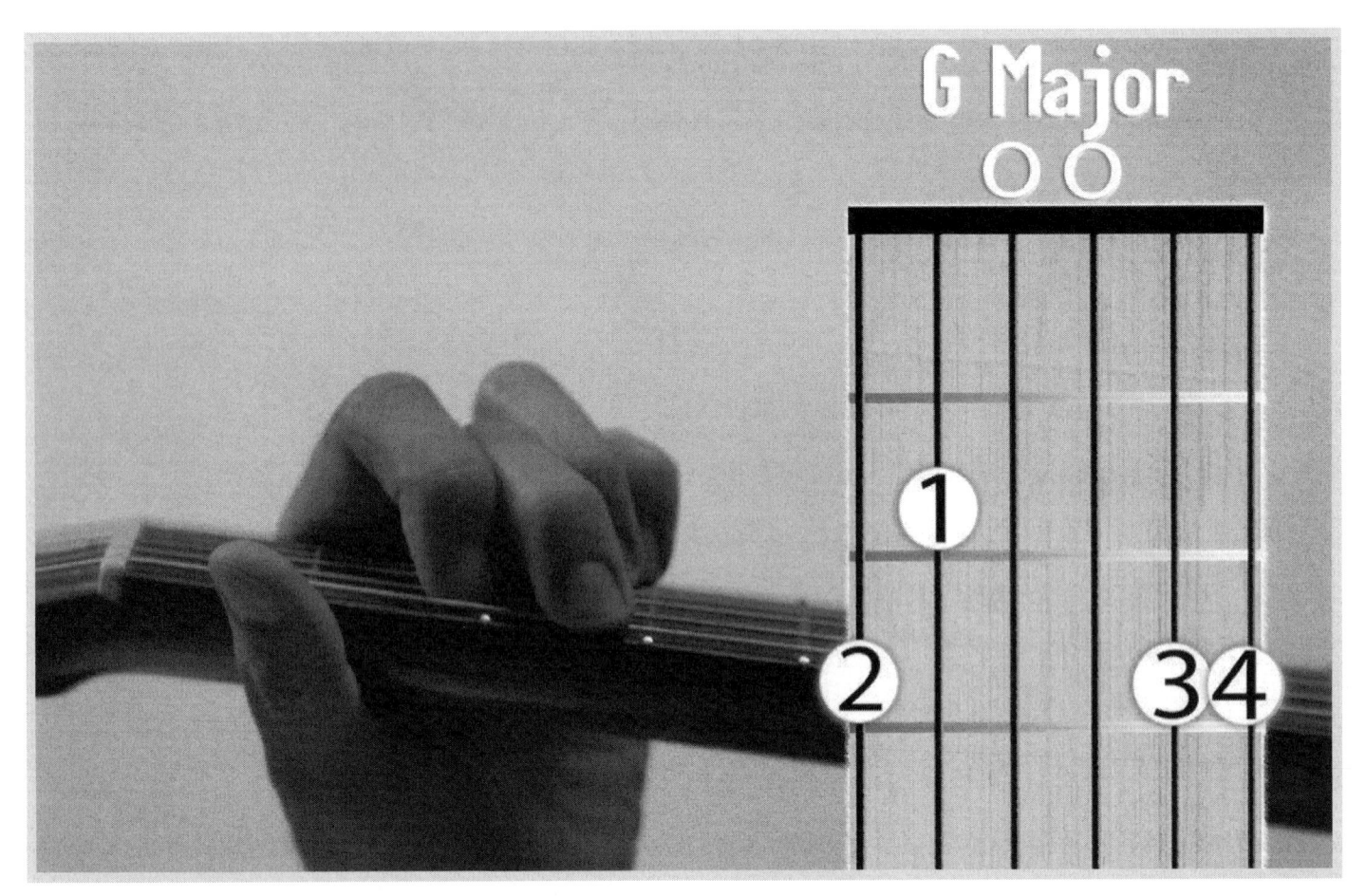

A Minor

73

E Major

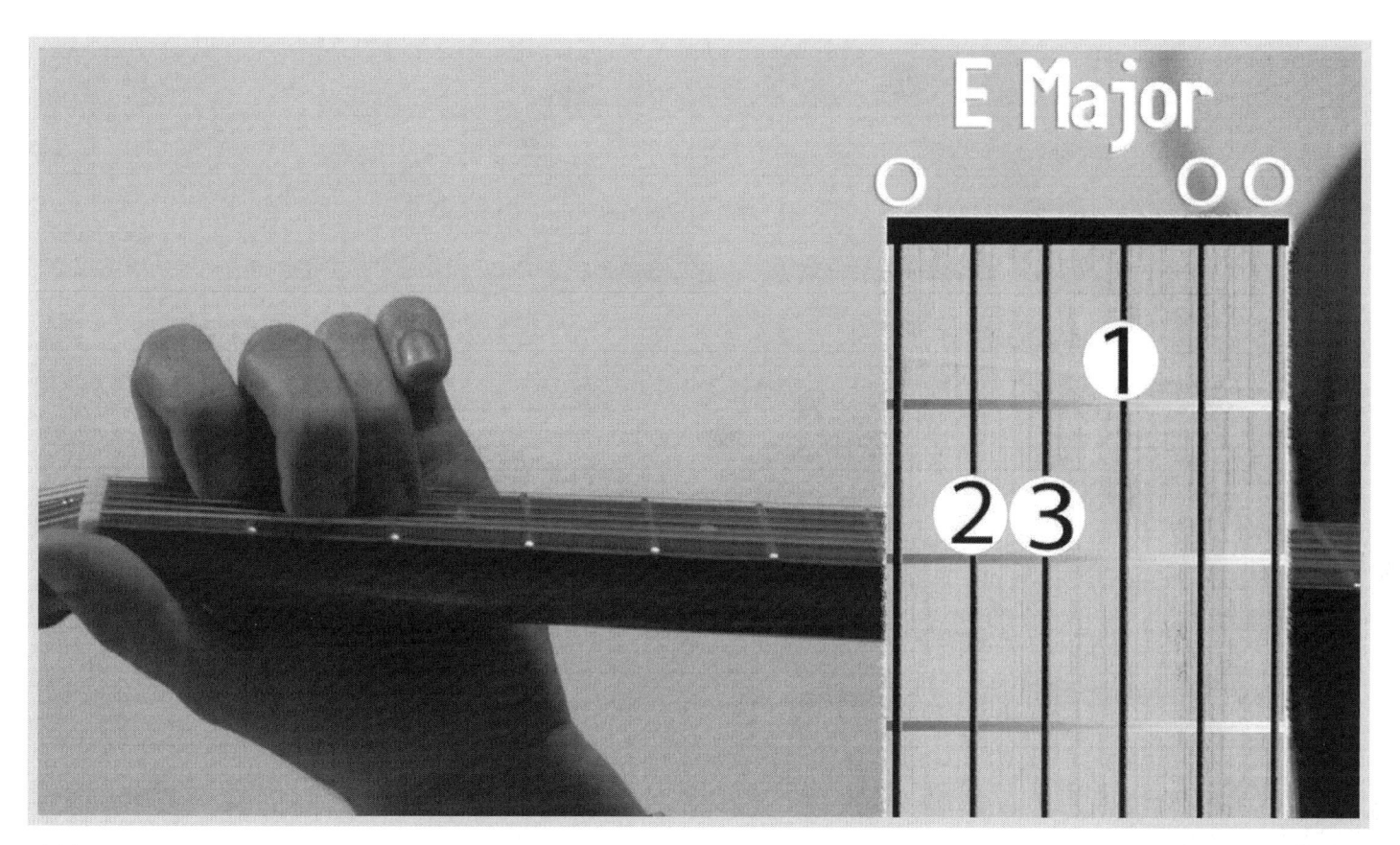

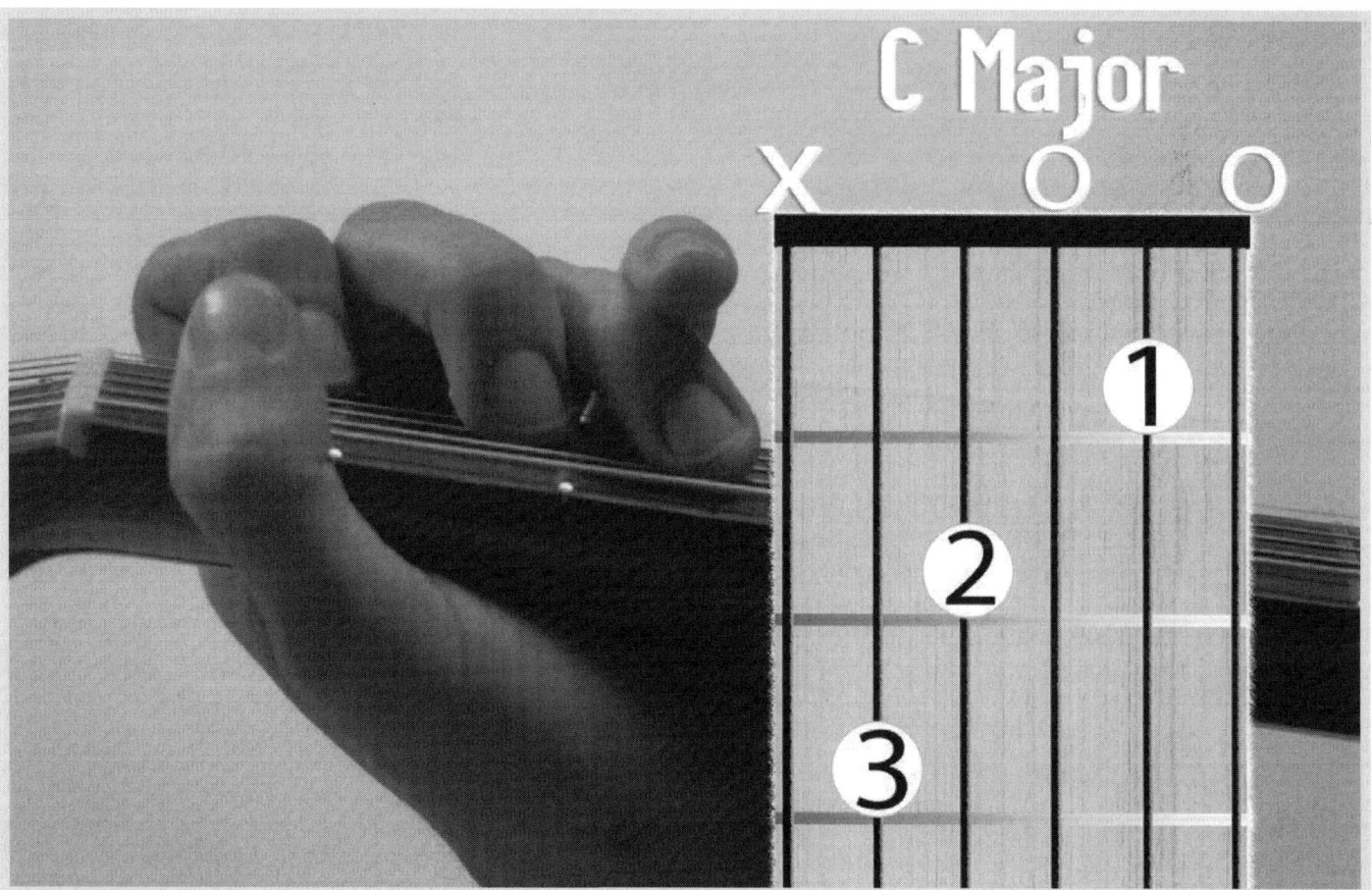

C Major

Here are the chord diagrams of all the chords I would suggest you get memorized:

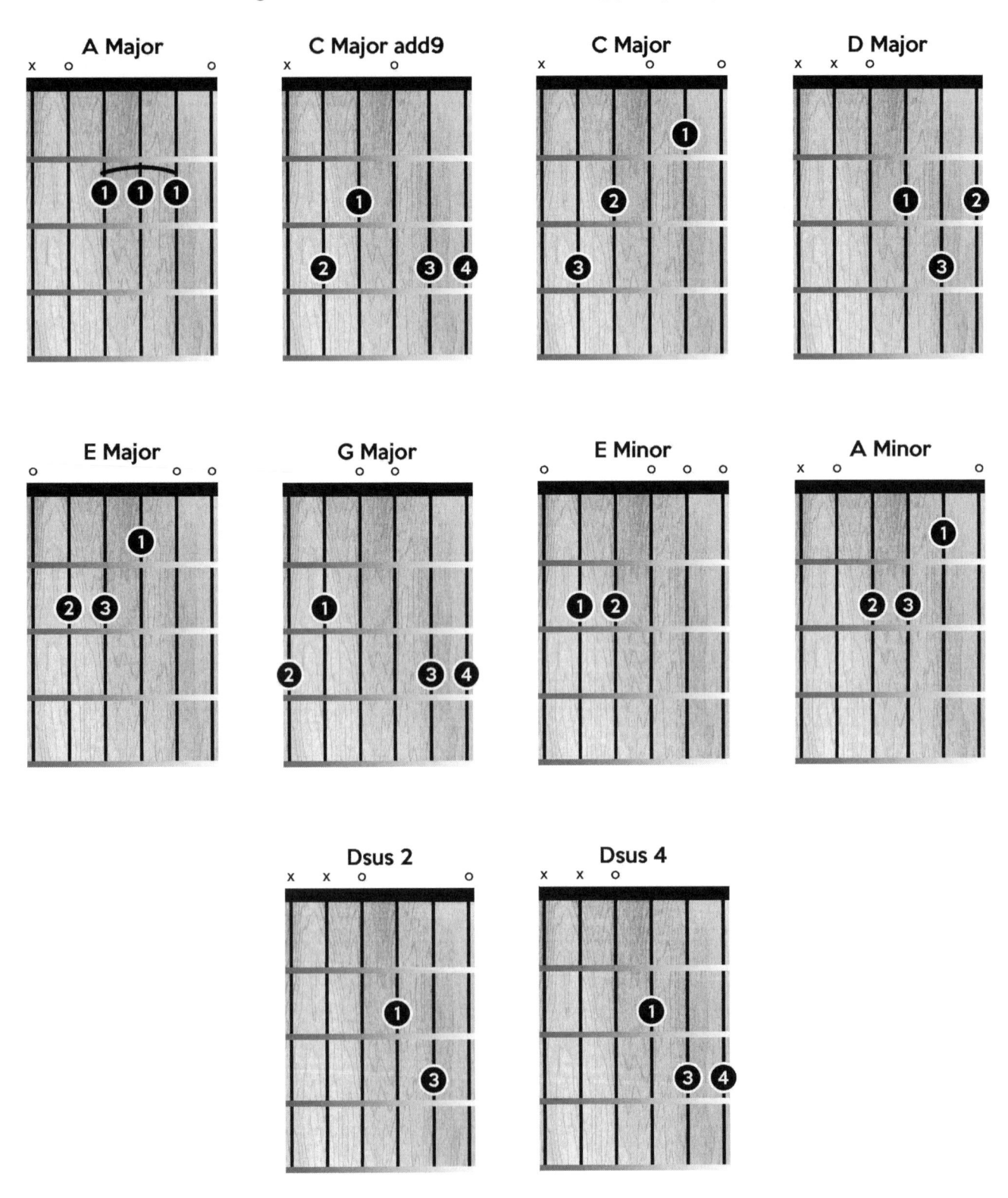

75

CHAPTER 19

AWESOME BEGINNER STRUMMING SONGS

Kids MGMT (pt.1)

"Kids" was released in 2008 by the US rock band MGMT. It charted high on US billboard and has been licensed for use by everything from video games and TV shows to advertizing Nokia phones.

This is the best song to start playing chords with… but there's a catch, the chords we are going to use are new! This is a versatile and fun chord progression. It is responsible for many other hit songs including Oasis's "Wonderwall", The Cranberries "Zombie", Green Day's "Boulevard of Broken Dreams", CCR's "Who'll stop the rain" and The Beatles "Yesterday".

Going between these chords is so easy, some fingers don't even move! These reasons are why this is a great song to work on while you continue to practice your major and minor chords.

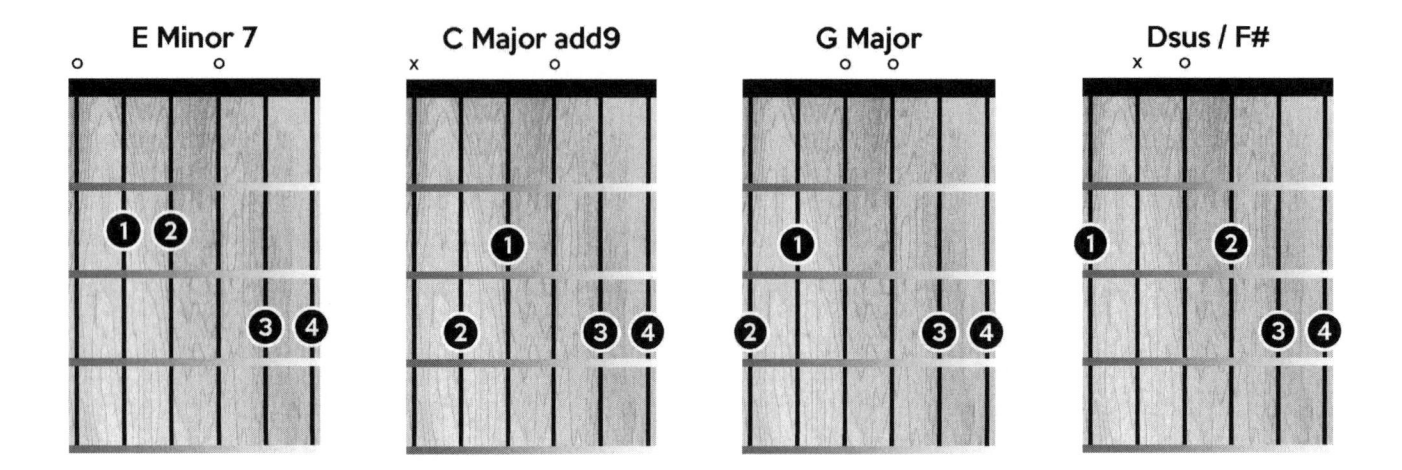

I bet you can see the similarities to other chords we have learned. What do you notice about the 3rd and 4th fingers? Yup, they are on each and every chord! So you're actually only moving your 1st and 2nd finger. Start by sticking the fingering for these chords in the progression shown and strum each one of them out.

Next, we will talk about how to strum and switch between these chords.

To play in key with the song you will need a capo placed on your 2nd fret. A capo must be placed straight and moderately close to the fret.

In the Dsus/F# you will see in the tab not to play your A string. Your first finger is already playing the string above, so flattening it down just until it touches will mute the string you don't want to play.

CHAPTER 20

AWESOME BEGINNER STRUMMING SONGS

Kids MGMT (pt.2)

This is one of the most jam packed lessons yet! We're now going to go over the right hand and strum patterns.

We have great sounding chords here that have a lot of similarities between them. We're going to play "Kids" but most importantly, I'm going to break down for you exactly how pro guitar players switch chords. And specifically, how they do it so effortlessly.

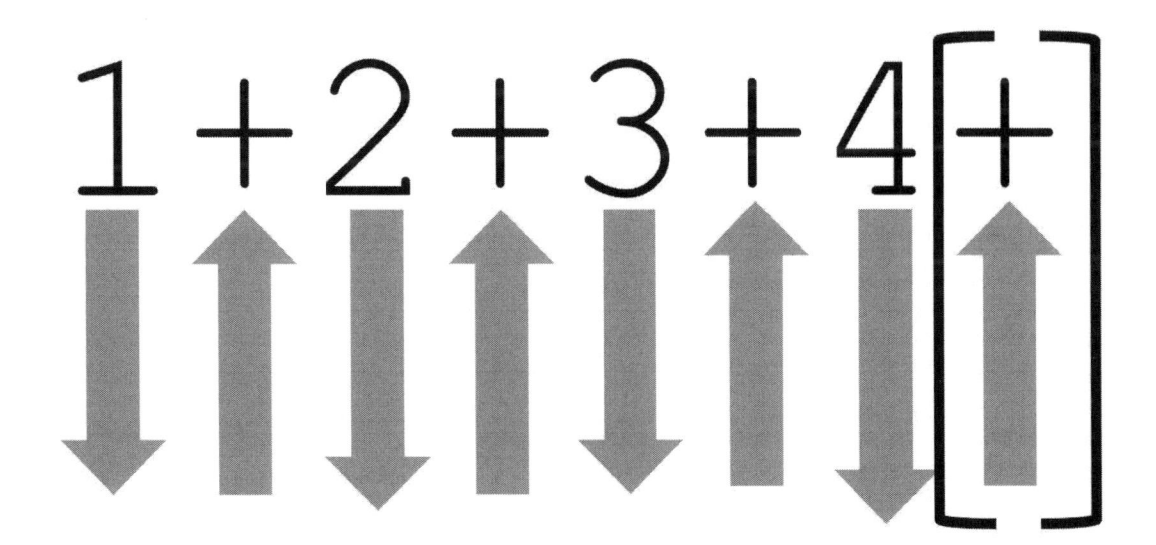

1 + 2 + 3 + 4 +
↓ ↑ ↓ ↑ ↓ ↑ ↓ ↑

Let's take a look at the strum pattern. Firstly, this is just showing you which direction to strum. You're either going to be strumming downwards or upwards. So, down and up arrows...cool!

The numbers on top are the rhythmic breakdown. The "+" symbol we read as "and". So if you were to read out "1+2+3+4+" that you see in the diagram, you're going to translate that and say "1 **AND** 2 **AND** 3 **AND** 4 **AND**". Try saying that out loud in a consistent rhythm and say it 4 times.

Rock/Pop music is generally in groupings of 4. Think about a drummer that's clicking his sticks together before a band kicks into a tune - "1, 2, 3, 4!". Groupings of 4 is what we connect easily with as humans listening to music. It's what we tap our feet to, bob our heads to and dance to.

So what we're doing here with this basic strum pattern is strumming all the numbers (1,2,3,4) with down strokes and all the "+" or "ands" with up strokes. Strum all the way through the strings, back and forth (up and down).

We're playing "8th notes" which means there is 2 strums per beat.

Starting with a downstroke and following with an upstroke, play through the progression. Each chord gets a total of 8 strums. Down up, down up, down up etc… Just like in the diagram.

Here are those chords again. Follow them left to right and strum each 8 times.

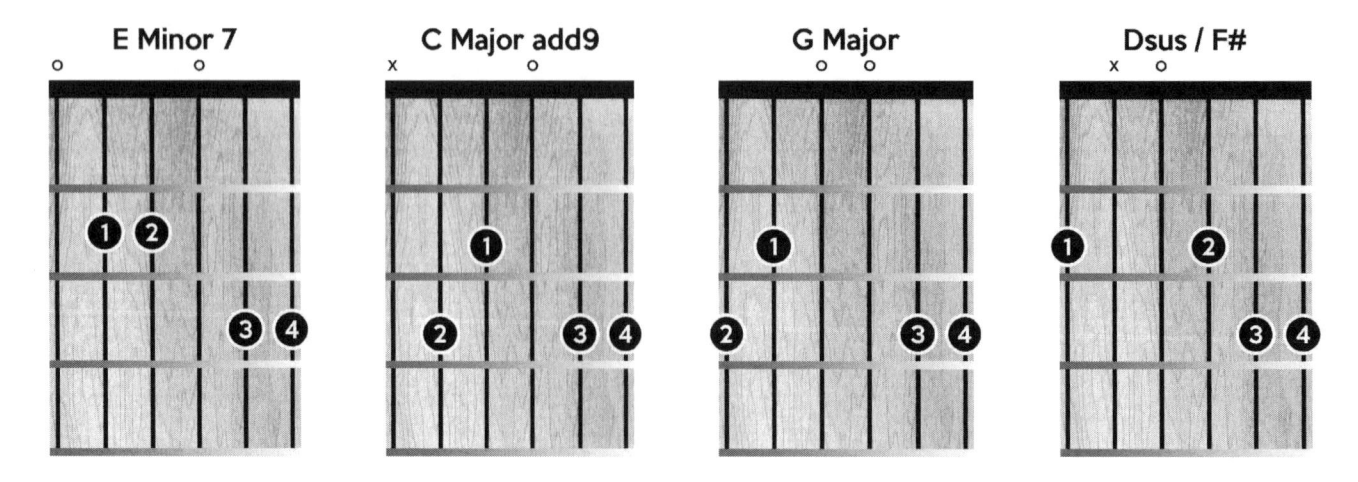

E Minor 7   **C Major add9**   **G Major**   **Dsus / F#**

The Big Secret To Changing Chords

Are you finding there's a big delay switching chords? Let's fix that.

This is probably the biggest thing guitar students find challenging. As far as I know, I've never seen switching chords taught in the way I'm about to share with you here… this is one of the secrets that professionals use to sound great.

I'm going to introduce you to a Will Ripley guitar teaching technique called the "upstroke bracket".

The "1st beat" is the most important beat to strum, so we need to have our chord ready prior to strumming it! We're only humans, so we need to leave each chord early to hit the next chord in time.

Let's refer back to the 1+2+3+4(+) diagram. We've talked about the downstrokes and upstrokes and sure enough, the last strum is an upstroke with a bracket around it.

Here's what you do (and I know this is going to sound crazy) - You're going to lift off the fingers on your left hand and continue strumming during the change. Yes - that means your going to be strumming some open strings.

We have to find time in the song to get our fingers quickly get to the next chord. By doing this, we can connect with the next chord in time for its first strum so we don't miss the chord change!

Try it out slow - it might sound a bit weird, but just work on lifting your fingers off and simultaneously strumming the open strings on that last upstroke (the "and" of 4).

These are great chords to practice this technique on because our 3rd and 4th fingers can actually just stay in the same spot.

Let's Make It Even Easier

You can also just take a Cadd9 and G Maj chord and switch back and forth between these 2 chords. This is an EXCELLENT way to practice this technique because as you probably know by now, these 2 chords are very similar in shape. Plus, they sound great together.

Here's this technique in action. As you can see, my 3rd and 4th fingers are glued to the fretboard, but I'm lifting off on my 1st and 2nd fingers at the same time as I'm doing the upstroke (the 8th strum).

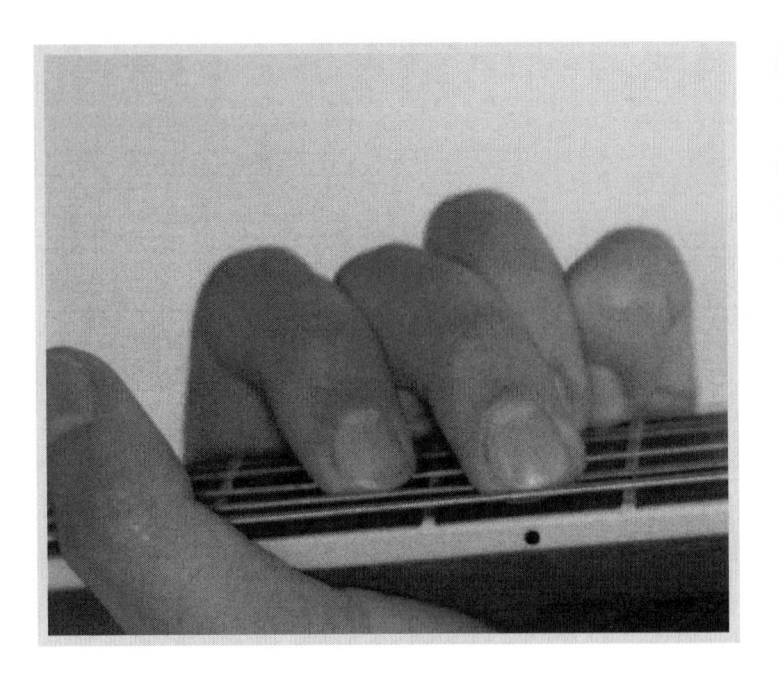

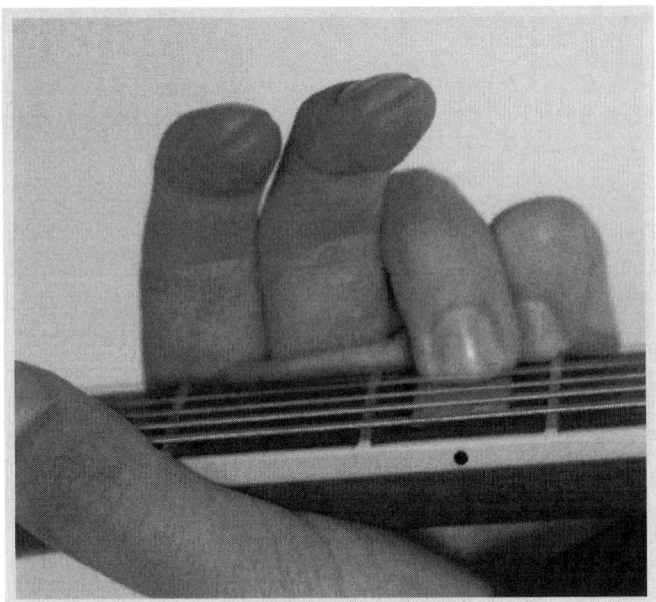

CHAPTER 21

HOW TO STICK CHORDS QUICKLY & REMEMBER THEM FOREVER

The S's

When you're first learning chords, it takes some time and concentration to get your fingers into position. The S's are the best way to start building that muscle memory you need to move quickly from chord to chord. Starting out with a C major chord...

1. **Stretch** - With your palm resting comfortably on the back of the neck, extend your fingers out so your hand is open and ready to go.

2. **Simultaneous Stick** - Slowly allow all of your fingers to fall into position at the same time. This is the best way to start

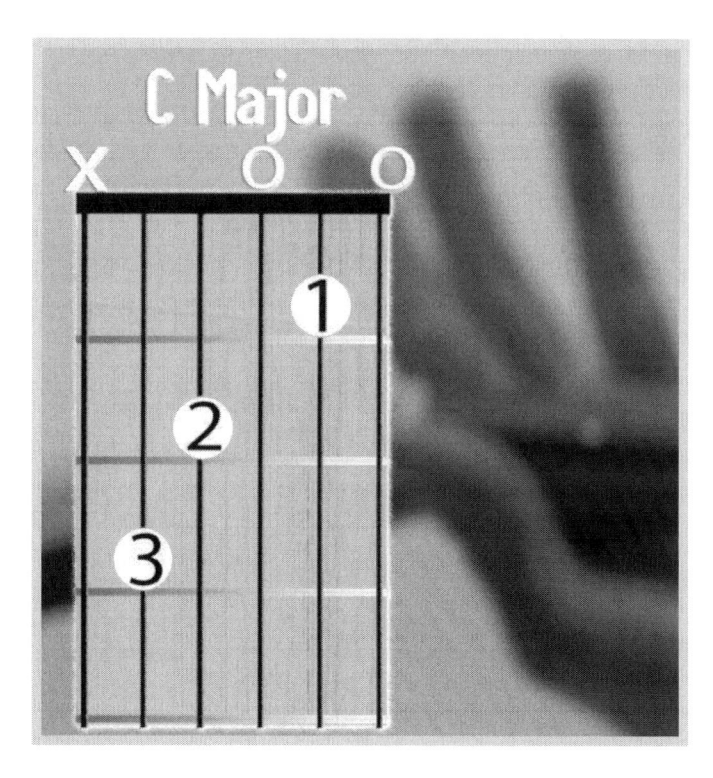

building that muscle memory you need to move quickly from chord to chord.

3. **Strum** - Arpeggiate the chord (strum through one string at a time) and make sure every note played is clear and continues to ring.

4. **Say it** - Say the name of the chord out loud. This will help lock it into memory.

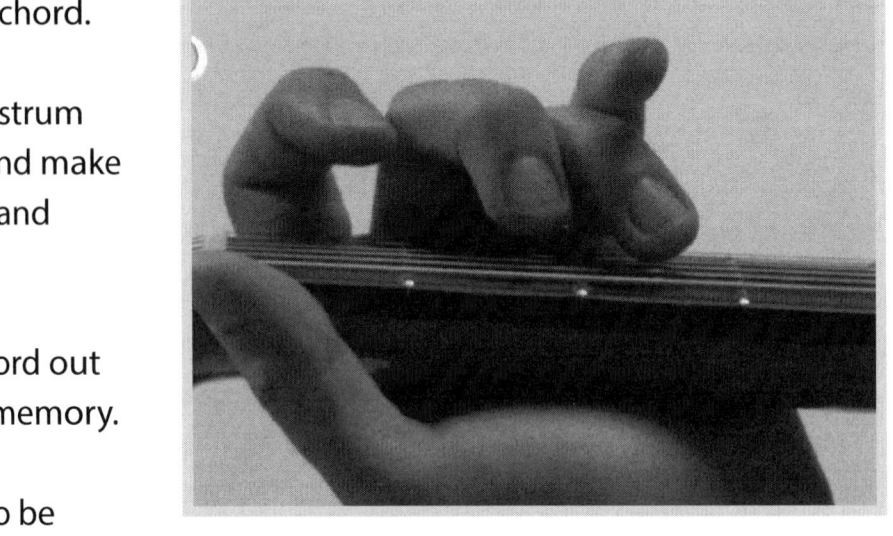

Songs are definitely the fun way to be learning chords and playing guitar. Chords are tough, but if you're dedicated and really want to get these chords going, this is going to be the best way get your fingers sticking every time into these shape.

By practicing just the first 2 S's (stretching your fingers and sticking the chord) back and forth quickly will be of huge benefit.

WHAT EVERY **GREAT GUITARIST** IN HISTORY HAS DONE & WHY YOU MIGHT CONSIDER DOING IT TOO

What is it that turns people into amazing guitarists? There are so many resources that are competing for our attention these days. Whether it's paying for DVD's, books, membership sites, or YouTube lessons, there are a ton of resources out there to learn guitar (much of which is free!). I've even seen people online dissing guitarists calling them lazy if they take 1-on-1 lessons because there's so much free content available online. There are even video games that claim to be "the best way to learn guitar" these days… so really, what's the key to unlocking your favorite songs, styles and techniques?

A large piece of the puzzle is that we all learn differently; We all have different learning 'modalities'. For example, take two similar people who want to learn the guitar. Plunk them in front of the same instructional video series and they will progress at very different rates. It doesn't mean that one of them is a slow learner or incapable, it just means that video instruction is more effective for one person than the other. When it comes to learning guitar, there is no "one size fits all" answer.

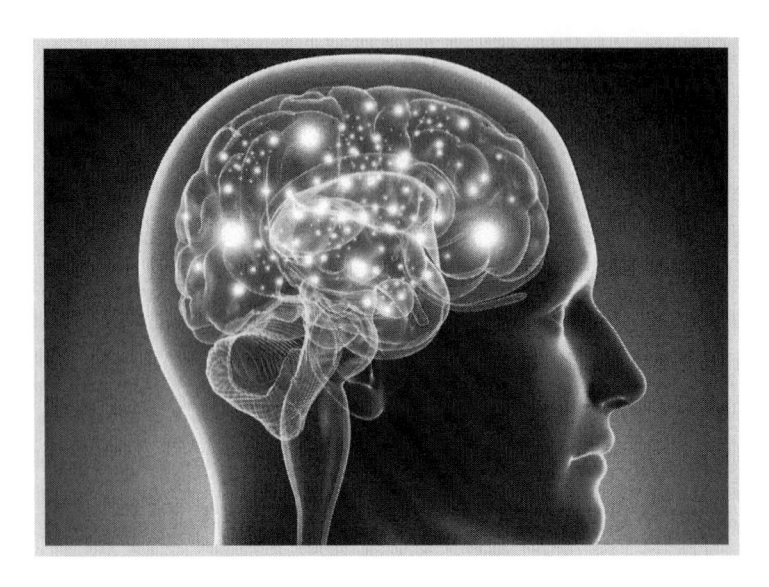

I'm also calling foul on all the people that say they taught themselves. I'm not discrediting all the time they spent practicing and their passionate dedication, I'm just saying that there were resources and knowledge that initially got them started.

Let me tell you a secret. **I still seek out guitar lessons**.

But Will!? You have been a professional guitarist and teacher for years!? Why do you need to take lessons?

Because this is about finding the best way to move forward, especially when you feel like you're trying your best and still not advancing. Additionally, with a good instructor, guitar lessons can be the most enjoyable way to learn. Here are the answers to the 4 big challenges and roadblocks people have when seeking out lessons.

Pride

It is very discouraging when you feel like you should be able to figure things out on your own. Let's talk about how some of the world's best guitarists have learned - The legendary Jimi Hendrix was finding his tricks from blues guitarists after their shows. At 17 years old he would hang outside of clubs, with his guitar in the early hours, begging these guys to teach him their riffs!

Randy Rhoades, known as one of the best guitarists this world has seen, would take private guitar lessons when he was at the height of his career playing packed stadiums with Ozzy Osbourne!

Slash from Guns N' Roses has about the closest to "teaching yourself" as it gets. In his biography, he talked about finding a rock guitar techniques book that he really connected with. This book taught him most of his foundational knowledge on riffs and soloing. But even this story - can we really say that Slash "taught himself"? It sure sounds like this book that written by someone who knew more than him (at the time at least) sure helped.

When Paul McCartney and John Lennon were trying to learn the guitar, they heard about some barber far across town who knew some new chords. They drove out to where he was and ended up learning the 'B7'; a chord that ended up in many famous Beatles songs. Those Liverpool boys were dedicated.

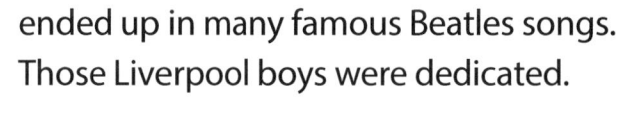

So, certainly there were no YouTube videos, membership sites, video games or DVD programs happening in this era. Can you see how some of the world's most famous guitar players have utilized the knowledge and experience of OTHER people to get their guitar playing to new levels?

Trust

You need to go to someone who can show you the ropes on your favourite styles, songs and guitar techniques. They need to be dedicated to your success, engaging and fun to take lessons with! You need to ask around and do a little research. It can be as simple as preparing some questions to ask your potential instructor to see if they would be a good candidate.

4 lessons with someone is usually a good indicator of the value you'll get. If you're trying

out a teacher and he's not pumping you up or helping you get to that next level, change your approach by changing your teacher.

There will always be some trial and error, but going through this process to find a great teacher will always be the fastest route to get your skills where you want them to be.

Time

You're not going to become a rockstar from one lesson... and just getting yourself there and back home can take over an hour! This is about the value of YOUR time. One solution is that you find a teacher that inspires you within your area. You can set up a time that works well for both of you, grab your guitar and have a great time hanging out with someone that will support you in getting to that next level.

The other solution is taking 1-on-1 webcam lessons from a professional online. This approach allows you to have your lesson, with none of the travel time. You can be anywhere in the world and with an internet connection, be getting 1-on-1 instruction from a professional guitarist at a convenient time. Many teachers offer this service and it works even better than you'd imagine.

I personally have taught hundreds of hours via webcam and am very used to the technology. Although I can't speak for every guitar teacher out there, I can confidently say that my 1-on-1 webcam lessons are just as effective as in-person sessions. Technology is becoming a very valuable tool that you can use to get better at guitar quickly, without having to leave your house.

Money

Let's face it. We don't want to spend our hard earned dough on a waste of time. We all have bills to pay and top level guitar instructors usually charge somewhere between $45-$75/hr. Some people think this seems like a lot and then they will happily spend $2,500 on a nice Gibson Les Paul.

At $50/hr you could get 50 hours (yes, FIFTY hours) of 1-on-1 time with a pro instructor. Just imagine what that would do for your guitar playing. You would absolutely get an incredible transformation of your musical ability - without a doubt!

This comes down to priorities and any guitarist who wants to quickly and easily play their favorite songs, styles and techniques should absolutely prioritize a series of lessons with a good instructor at some point in their pursuit of guitar playing.

In Conclusion

Lastly, I want to share with you my first memories of taking a guitar lesson. I was nine years old and after wanting to play the guitar for a long time, my mother got me some lessons. My instructor was an amazing guitar player. I would pass him my guitar at the beginning of the lessons, he would make sure it was in tune and always play a little bit. That was my favourite part of the lesson, I would watch as MY GUITAR would produce these incredible sounds and could see what was possible.

Unfortunately, the lessons were really uninspiring otherwise and I almost quit the guitar for good! I was moving at that time and was super lucky to get an awesome guitar teacher in the city we moved to. This teacher who helped me discover awesome techniques and my love for the blues and rock.

Throughout my entire career of playing guitar, 1-on-1 lessons have played an integral role in my guitar playing. From being a full time teacher myself, I know what kind of results are possible with 1-on-1 lessons and when you zoom out and take a look at history, you see the important role of guidance from others plays when it comes to learning an instrument.

Just like blues and country music influenced rock n' roll, a guitarist that has more experience and knowledge can accelerate your learning pace on the guitar in a huge way.

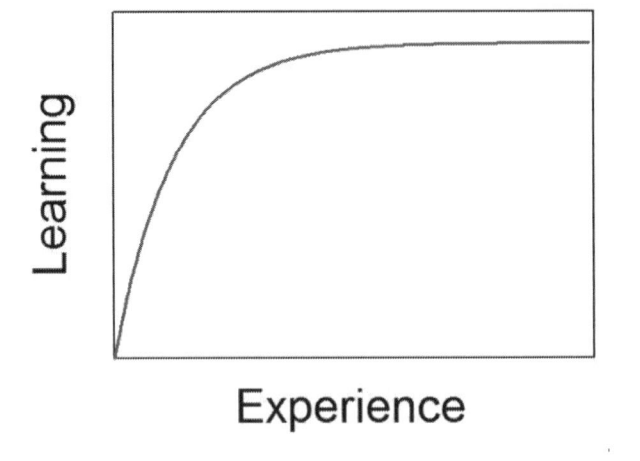

It doesn't matter what your approach is. It's just about finding what works for you. Most people respond very well to 1-on-1 guidance with a real person in real time. But I also encourage you to hit up YouTube, buy a book, get a video series, or commit to taking a lesson a week for a month or 2! Find your best learning modality with the guitar. Achieving your goals on the guitar is possible when you have support in taking right steps.

Will Ripley

TIRED OF YOUR SLOW PROGRESS WITH THE GUITAR?

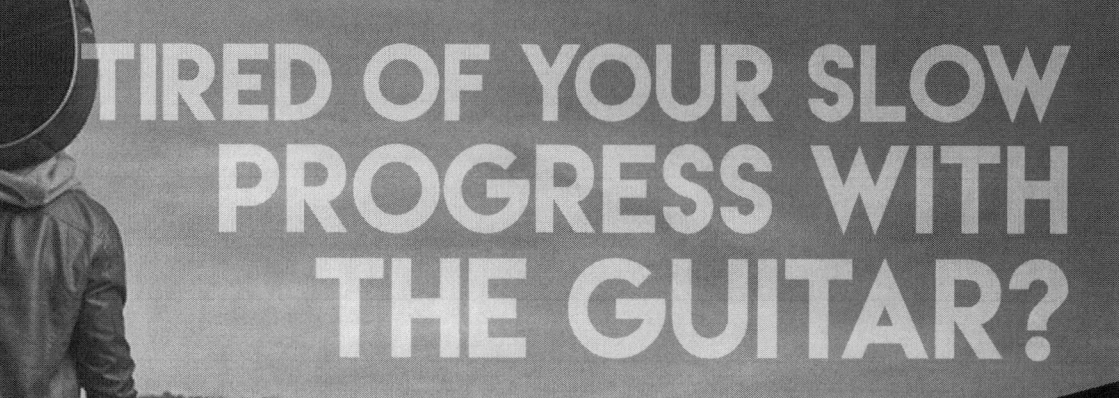

Supercharge Your Learning Speed With 1-on-1 Lessons. Get access to a pro teacher from Campfire Guitar Star, from the comfort of your own home, in real-time

GET A FREE INTRO SESSION!

- Advance your guitar skills easily and quickly while having a blast
- A guitar, a computer with an internet connection, and the hunger to get better is all you need
- You'll have the ability to record your lessons
- 1-on-1 guitar lessons right from the comfort of your own home
- Get the ability to play and jam with others and perform for your friends and family
- Learn the techniques, theory and magic behind all your favourite songs and styles

Apply Now At
http://www.CampfireGuitarStar.com/1on1Webcam
and get a free introductory lesson

Rather Connect By Phone? Call us.
1-855-974-7539

CHAPTER 22

PARADISE CITY

Paradise City

Released in 1987 by Guns 'N Roses on their first album "Appetite for Destruction". It has since sold approximately 30 million copies worldwide! "Paradise City" is said to have been written by the band while they were all hanging out in the back of their rental van after a gig. Slash, their iconic guitarist, has said that this is his favorite Guns 'N Roses song. It's frequently played at sporting events and has been covered by many other famous musicians… and even Tom Cruise.

The first chord is a G chord, but it looks a little different. Playing it in this formulation helps it ring and sound more open. It's also makes it very easy to switch between chords.

The next chord is a Cadd9 shape, but just missing that 1st finger. The 3rd shape as you can see, you just move that 2nd finger down one more string. This is basically acting as an F chord.

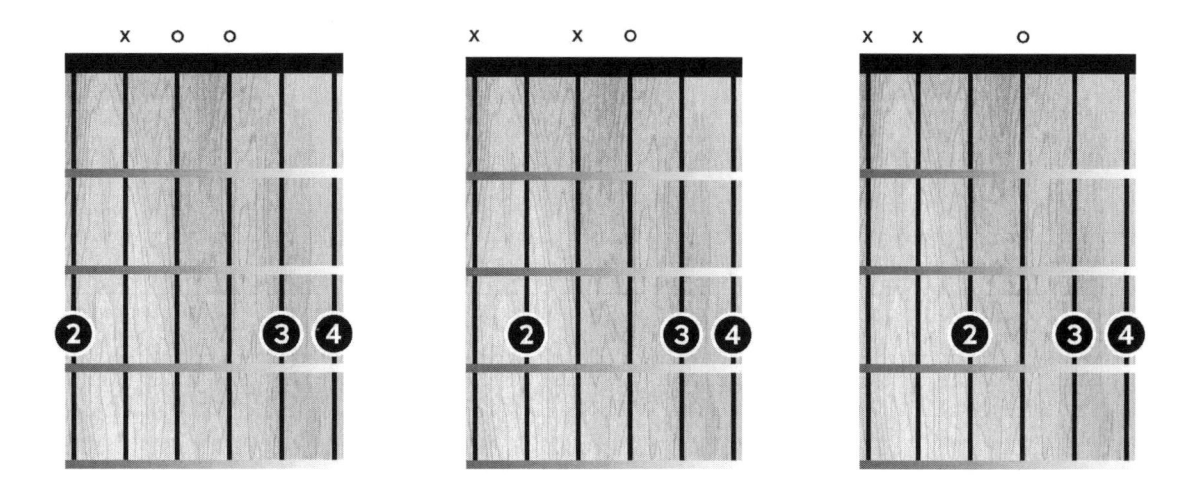

This is a super classic strum pattern and is another great song to practice the "bracketed upstrokes". Check out the strum pattern below and every time you see a bracketed strum, that is where you move your second finger to create the next chord.

Check the chord charts and use the techniques we've learned to make sure you're not playing the strings marked with an "X"

If the strum pattern is hard to "feel" - get logged in at CampfireGuitarStar.ROCKS and watch the video. Often once you hear the strum pattern or the rhythm, the arrows start to make a whole lot more sense

CHAPTER 23

FREE FALLIN'

Free Fallin'

Tom Petty is one of the best-selling musicians of all time. "Free Fallin'" was the title track to his debut solo album back in 1989 and is without a doubt, still his most famous song. It was written and recorded in just 2 days, and the lyrics reference a lot of places local to the San Fernando Valley in LA. This song still receives heavy radio play and has been featured in movies and has also been covered by many famous artists.

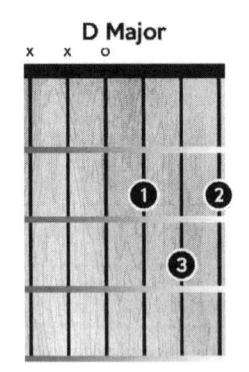

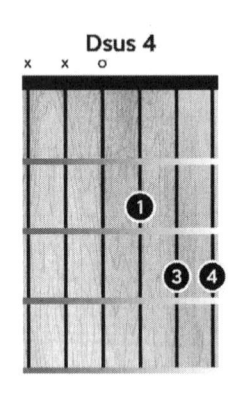

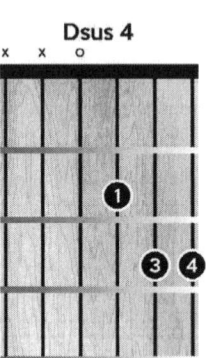

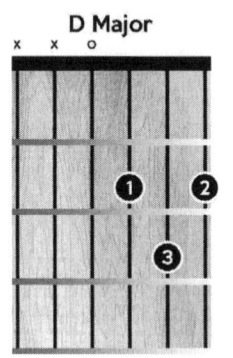

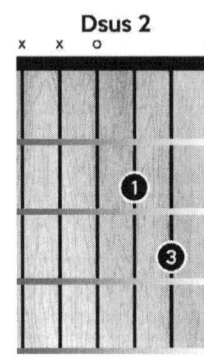

D Major — x x o
Dsus 4 — x x o
Dsus 4 — x x o
D Major — x x o
Dsus 2 — x x o o

Looking at the chord charts above, you can see that they are all variations of the D chord. The rest of the chords all say "sus" after them. "Sus" is in reference to "suspended". Listening to the sound gives you an unresolved or "suspended" feeling.

*Get a good angle on your fingers and make sure all your notes are ringing clear.
* To play in key with the original song, place your capo on the 3rd fret and transpose the chords accordingly.
*Once again, watch out for those "X" markings on the strings!

CHAPTER 24

SWEET CHILD O' MINE

Sweet Child O' Mine

Another huge hit off the Guns N' Roses "Appetite for Destruction" album with "Paradise City" was their third single, "Sweet Child O' Mine".

The song came about when Slash played the opening riff as a finger warmup exercise. Another band member from GnR started playing along and it became the only song of theirs to reach number one on the US charts! The studio version is played with the guitars tuned down a half step. This was something the band did often, possibly to accommodate Axl Rose to hit those high notes and for the guitars to get a lower, fuller sound.

This is often referred to as the "classic folk strum pattern". We will also be using the bracketed upstroke. This strum pattern is found in many songs including "Brown Eyed Girl" by Van Morrison and "For What It's Worth" by Buffalo Springfield. We teach these songs in our Acoustic Guitar Star program which is available through our website.

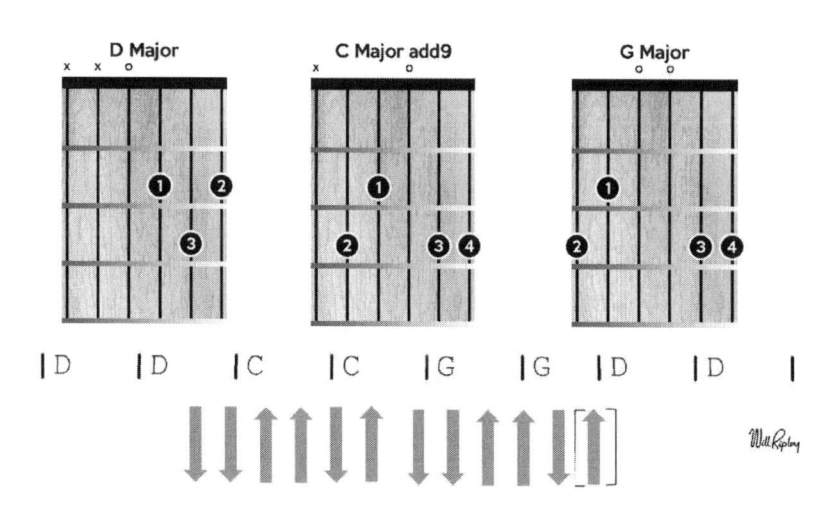

| D Major | C Major add9 | G Major |

| D | D | C | C | G | G | D | D |

A Very Important D Chord Switching Technique

It doesn't introduce any new chords, but when you change from the D to the C add9 make sure you get that pinky finger on the high e string!

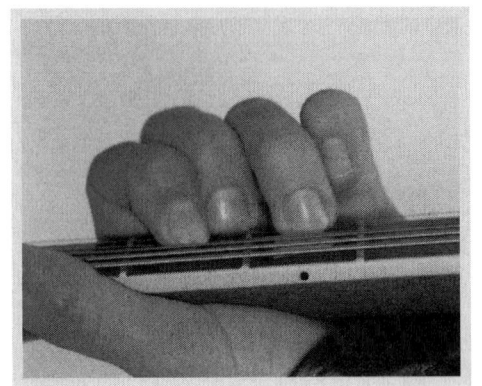

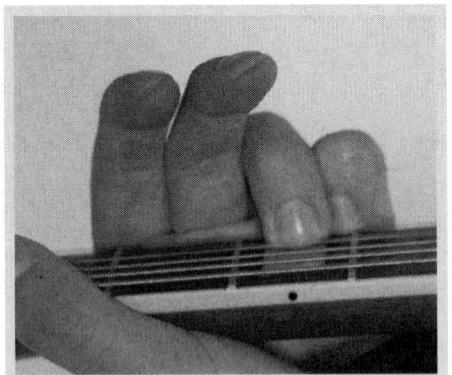

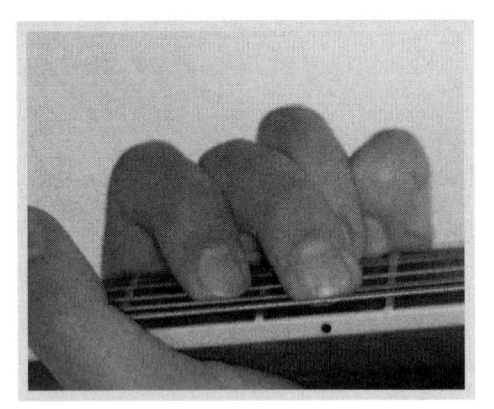

Step 1

Step 2

Step 3

- **Step 1:** Here we are strumming away on our D Chord:
- **Step 2:** Here's the position we will be in for the "bracketed upstroke". So instead of removing your fingers and playing open strings like I've taught you in previous lessons, when you're switching from a D chord to either a Cadd9 or G major, you'll want to ADD your pinky finger on the final strum like this:
- **Step 3:** Land on the Cadd9 or the G (depending on the song) for the first beat of the next bar.

Here are additional parts of the song:

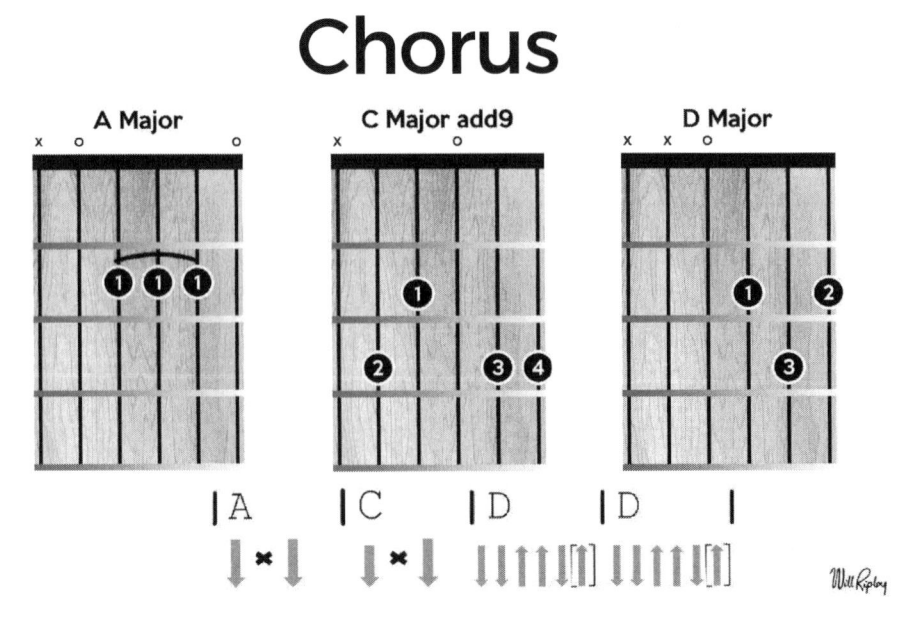

Chorus

Bridge (guitar solo happens over this part)

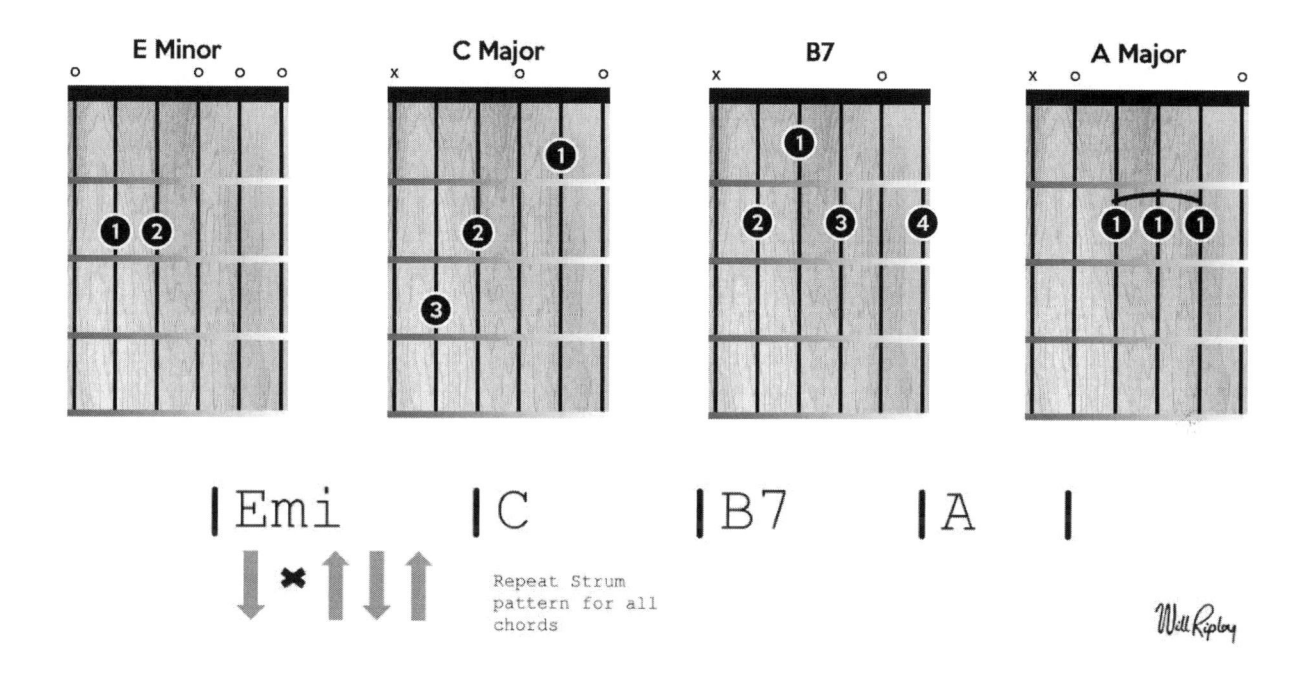

E Minor   **C Major**   **B7**   **A Major**

| Emi | C | B7 | A |

↓ ✗ ↑ ↑ ↓

Repeat Strum pattern for all chords

Will Ripley

CHAPTER 25

LEAVING ON A JET PLANE

Leaving On A Jet Plane

John Denver had been playing music in clubs after dropping out of school in 1963 and moving to LA. In 1966, he decided to make an album as a Christmas present friends and family. "Babe I Hate To Go" was a song on that album that was so popular, the very next year, it was released under the title "Leaving On A Jet Plane" by three different artists. The version by Peter, Paul & Mary became not only the most successful version of the song, but the band's biggest hit, holding the #1 spot in 1969.

Denver finally found mainstream success in 1971 with the song "Take Me Home, Country Roads", and continued to write hits from then on. Life after his music career spanned from political activism and humanitarian work to flying planes and working with NASA.

The chord progression starts by switching back and forth 3 times between G major and C major add 9. The strum pattern is the same as "Paradise city", it's just played slower. Keeping your 3rd finger on the third fret, use the bracketed up strokes to change chords.

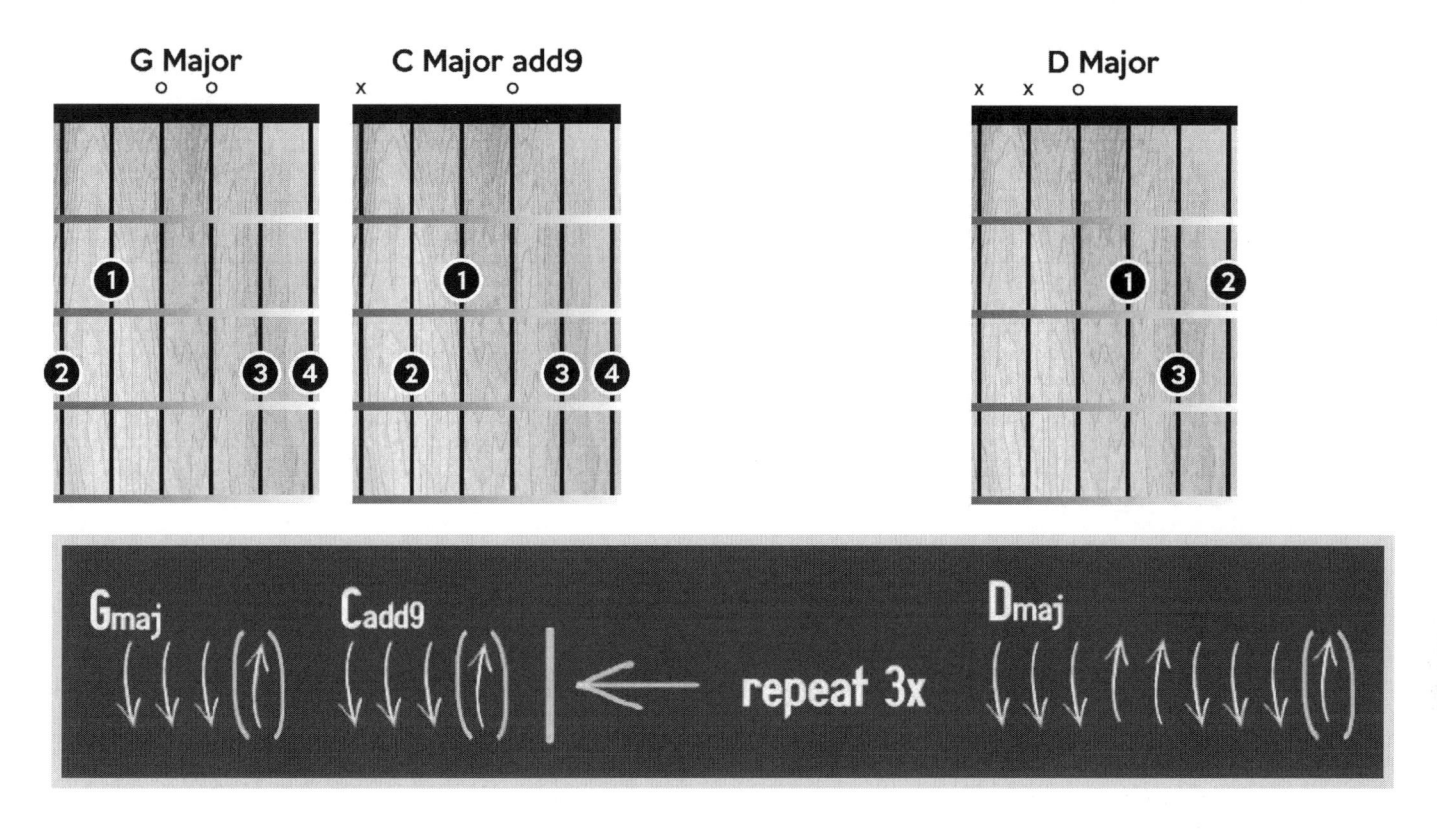

*Review the lesson on "Sweet Child O' Mine" to review the big secret for switching from a D major to a Cadd9 or G Major. You'll need to get your pinky finger down for that bracketed upstroke!

Be A Part Of The Legacy Of
ACOUSTIC GUITAR

Get Access To - "Acoustic Guitar Star" The Brand New Video Series From Campfire Guitar Star

Play Amazing Sounding Acoustic Guitar & Become Proficient In:

* Blues/Rock/Folk/Country/Pop
* Chord strumming
* Finger picking
* Advanced rhythmic techinques

Discover "Acoustic Guitar Star"
WWW.CAMPFIREGUITARSTAR.COM/ACOUSTIC

DON'T LIMIT YOURSELF
Login & Get All The Videos!

This Book Corresponds Directly To The Video Series.
Improve Your Likelihood Of Guitar Success By Combining
The Written Material & The Step-By-Step Video Instruction!

Register and Login At:
WWW.CAMPFIREGUITARSTAR.ROCKS

MODULE 6

BARRE CHORDS

PLAY EVERY MAJOR AND MINOR CHORD

CHAPTER 26

DISCOVER EVERY NOTE
ON THE GUITAR FRETBOARD (UNLOCK THE GRID)

Notes on the Fretboard

This is a big chapter. We're going to unlock your fretboard. You're going to be able to play the same major and minor chords in up to 3 different ways...without even thinking about it! Of course that last bit will take some practice... but I hope you find the idea of this to be motivating and exciting!

So, I'm going to show you how to find every single note on the guitar. We know the names of the strings (E, A, D, G, B, e), and these are the notes when the strings are played open. Say if you play the first fret of the E string - it's not longer an "E" note. We've just changed the pitch. That note now sounds different and altered. So, let's get into this easy-to-remember formula and unlock the mysterious guitar grid!

There are only 2 sets of notes that you need to remember:
*E to F
*B to C

This is important because they don't have a sharp (#) or a flat (b) between them. Every other note does.

In general musician terms, when you sharpen (#) a note it means you raise the pitch. Conversely, when you flatten (b) the note you're going to lower the pitch.

Let's talk about semitones and whole tones for a second. Getting a grip on this concept will deepen your knowledge for what we're about to get into.

On the guitar you can grab any ol' fret on any ol' string. Go ahead - grab any note. When you play a fret above that note, we just sharpened it (#), or "raised the pitch". Another way of saying it is we just "raised the pitch by a semitone". Now, if we are to go back to that original note we started on and play 1-fret lower, we just made it flat (b). We could also say that we just lowered the pitch by a semitone.

So 1 fret = 1 semitone. Got it?

Whole tones get the same treatment and breakdown, but whole tones are always 2 frets on the guitar.

1 whole tone = 2 frets. Ok?

Let's talk about the 1st fret of the E string again. Starting with your low E string and sharpening the pitch by one fret/semitone, you would play the 1st fret of the E string. Now we can reference the sets of notes above. The first one, (E to F) is exactly what is happening here. We just went from E to F! As you know, there is no sharp or flat between them. The next note up on your low E string is an F.

That bares repeating. The next note up on your low E string is an F.

Got it? Where do we go from here?

Now you're on the F, raise that pitch one more time and you'll be on the second fret of the low E string. Referencing the sets of notes again it seems as though we should now use a sharp or flat… but which one?

We're talking about raising the pitch of that 1st fret to the 2nd fret… so we're taking a F note and making it sharp. We end up with a F# - That's the note on the 2nd fret of the low E-string!

Again - the 2nd fret on the low E-string is a F#. Got it!

Ok, so It's a F#, but could it be something else too? Could the same note have 2 different names? Yes, check out this term called Enharmonics:

Enharmonics: "a note, interval, or key signature that is equivalent to some other note, interval, or key signature but "spelled", or named differently."

So let's just forget about enharmonics for a second and get back on the 2nd fret of the low E-string - the F#, right? What's the note 1 fret above that?

You want to ask yourself - "What's the letter after F in the alphabet?"

A, B, C, D, E, F, **G!**

Going up one more fret, you'll find a G.

Ok awesome, and hey, your G chord actually starts from that 3rd fret of the low E-string, doesn't it? Yup, no coincidence there!

Now that you're on your G - let's talk about lowering the pitch of the G. Like, if we were to make it "flat", what direction would we go? That's right, if we were to make the Gb, we'd just go ahead and go down 1-fret, back to the 2nd fret on the low E-string…wait a second… That note was F#, wasn't it?

F sharp (#) can also be called G flat (b). They are enharmonically the same note. Yup, F# = Gb.

Moving on, what is one note higher than the G? Raising the pitch of G by 1 semi-tone or fret will give you G#. What's one note higher than that? A. Ok, what about if we were to make A flat? Take A and lower it one fret. Same idea - G# = Ab which is the 4th fret of the low E-string.

Going up your strings, follow this same concept and fill out this blank fretboard diagram that you'll see here on this page. Grab a marker, pencil or pen and start filling this thing out!

Some Important Notes About This New Skill Of Yours

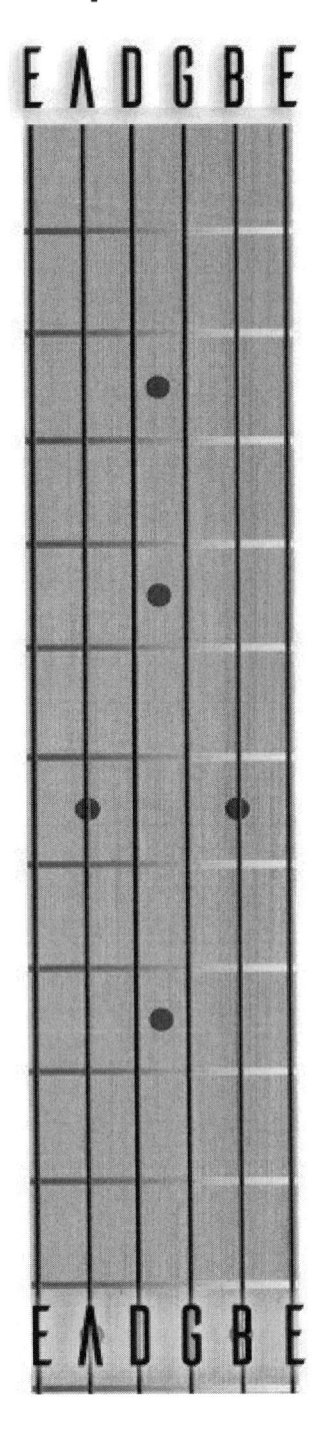

THE KEY: You'll notice that the blank fretboard diagram has the notes at the 12th fret written in. This is designed so that you cannot fail when filling this chord chart out. You'll notice that the notes at the 12th fret are E,A,D,G,B,e - just like your open strings. So this is where the notes repeat. As long as you fill out your chart and they line up at the 12th fret, you'll know you've filled out the chart correctly.

- *The musical alphabet goes A-G (A,B,C,D,E,F,G,A,B,C,D, etc...) but has sharps and flats between most of the notes.*
- *B-C and E-F don't have a sharp or flat between them.*
- *Music only has 12 notes!*

1. A
2. A#/Bb
3. B
4. C
5. C#/Db
6. D
7. D#/Eb
8. E
9. F
10. F#/Gb
11. G
12. G#/Ab

CHAPTER 27

INTRO TO BARRE CHORDS

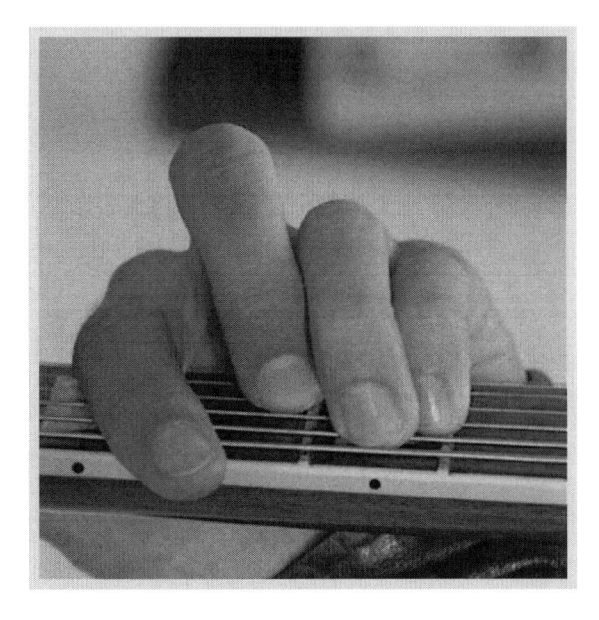

Barre chords are an **essential** next stage of playing guitar after you get your open position major and minor chords down. Many people try to play barre chords too early into playing guitar and get very frustrated. If you have never played one before, they can be a bit tricky. The good news is, we're going to integrate barre chords into your guitar playing from sources that you're already familiar with!

I would really encourage you to get your riffs, power chord songs and chord strumming down at least a bit before you attempt barre chords.

A huge advantage of playing barre chords is so you can play any major and minor chord in up to 3 different ways without even thinking about it!

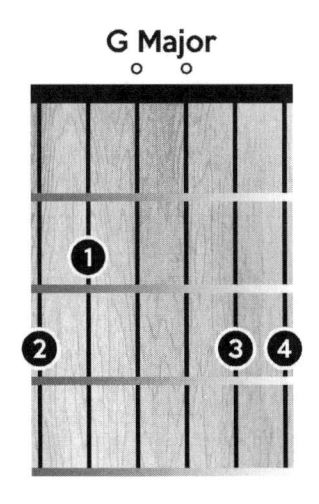

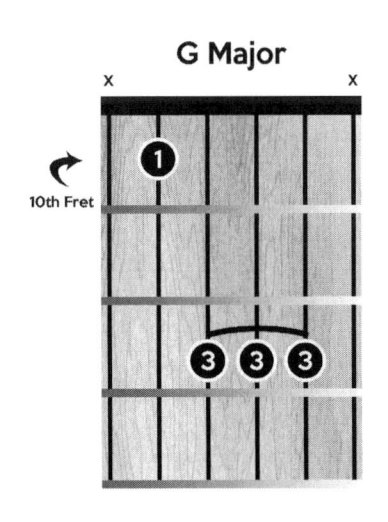

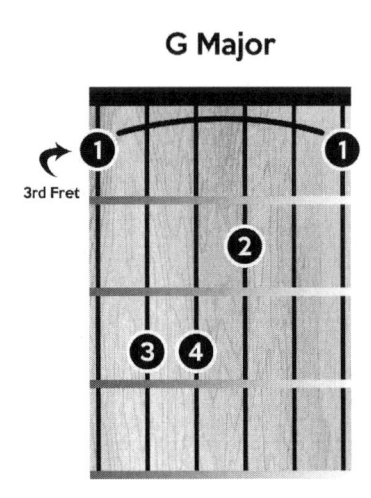

G Major

G Major (10th Fret)

G Major (3rd Fret)

106

Imagine this skill being put to use when you see a G major chord in a song (which as you can probably guess is pretty often). When all this knowledge is put together, you'll be able to find a G major chord in your open position **AND** in **2 different** barre chord positions! Yup, 3 different ways of playing the same chord.

I have to mention this before we go any further... These technique will also help you orientate yourself around the guitar so you can have a deeper understanding of keys and scales when it comes to ripping solos.

So, the name "barre" comes from "barring" which is a technique using **one finger** to hold down **multiple strings** at the same time.

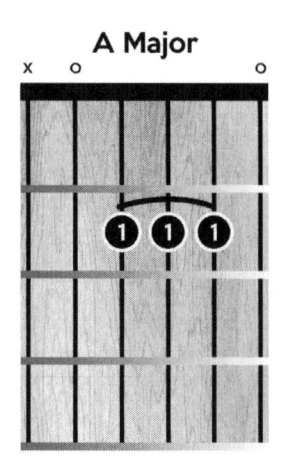

Remember, we ran into this barring concept when learning how to play an A Major chord? The A Major barre held down the 3 notes on one fret. The strings were right next to each other so we're making it easier to play at the same time!

Just like an athlete increases his potential by going to the gym, you need to develop the muscles in your hand with practice. If you've been finding time to practice every day, even if it's just picking up the guitar and strumming for 5 minutes, it won't be long before you get a great sounding barre every time.

What we will discuss in the next couple of chapters is the application of barre chords using our knowledge from open chords, power chords and notes on the fretboard so you can literally play **any** major or minor chord!

Of course, as you practice these, make sure all the strings are sounding out and **the "S's"** will really help you with barre chords as well.

1. **Stretch** Your fingers out (The ready position - or like you're switching from another chord).
2. **Simultaneously stick** the chord (let all your fingers fall into place at the same time into the chord formation).
3. **Strum** out the chord (make every note crystal clear).
4. **Say** the chord out loud (it will help you memorize the root note and chord formation).

TIPS TO PLAY CRYSTAL CLEAR BARRE CHORDS FOR LIFE

Barre chords can be extremely difficult for first timers. I want to show you how to get these chords faster and sounding a lot better.

The first common mistake I see a lot of people doing, is that they've got their first finger perfectly straight on the fret of the guitar. I know how you might think that's how it's supposed to be played - you see it written down somewhere and think 'that means I need to put my finger down exactly flush to get a good sound'.

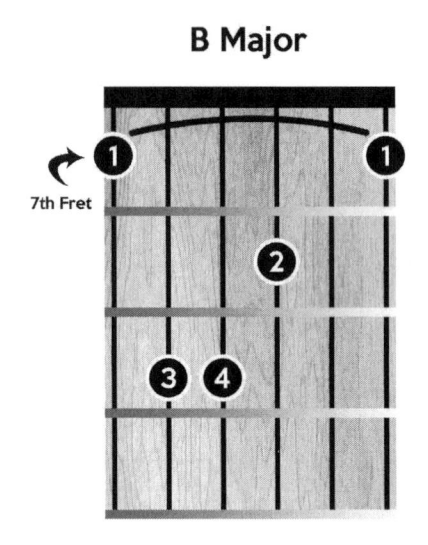

B Major

For example - This chord chart doesn't tell you ANYTHING about hanging your finger over the edge of the neck - It's common for people to think the opposite.

Without your finger comfortably gripping a full barre, that nasty, buzzy sound comes out or certain notes just won't have enough pressure on them.

Pull your barring finger up so it's like you're pointing at yourself and hanging over the edge of the guitar. This will do 2 things:

1. Adjust your wrist at a 90* angle
2. Get the tip of your finger hanging over the edge so it's no longer 'flush'

The big thing here is getting that finger so it's hanging way over the wood. My pointer finger is hanging so far over the neck, the edge of the fretboard lines up at the first knuckle! I can actually wrap my finger around there a little bit if I wanted to. Check it out for yourself, this tip alone has helped a ton of students play barre chords almost instantly.

The 90* Wrist Angle For Tough Riffs, Chords & Scales

When you reach for the low strings, it's a bit of a stretch. I want you to put your wrist on a hard 90 degree angle. This is like upside down T-Rex dinosaur's little arms! That's going to help you get those bar chords standing up a little straighter because with your wrist slammed on that angle, it gives you more leverage. So, as soon as my wrist is in this 90 degree position, this immediately makes all my fingers stand up straight. Additionally it supports the idea of your first finger hanging over the edge of the guitar neck.

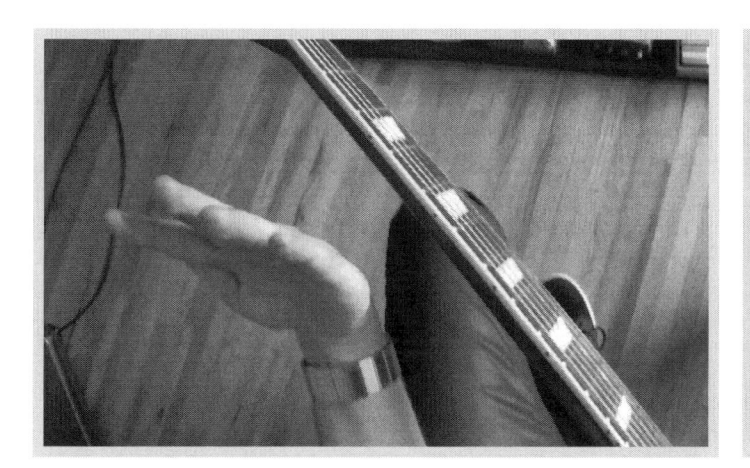

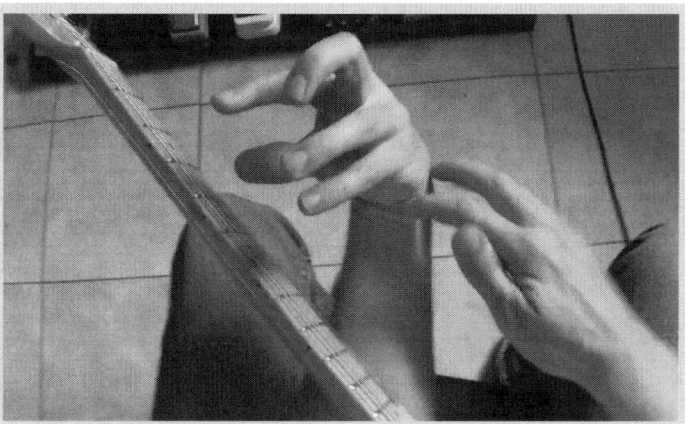

You should expect a nice, clean sound going on! This technique works great for those scales and riffs that require big stretches with you hand.

Squeeze It With Your Thumb

Now, the last thing I want to point out, is your thumb. This thumb has a huge amount of strength and is a big determining factor to squeezing out clean notes. This is where all of your strength comes from when building these barre chords.

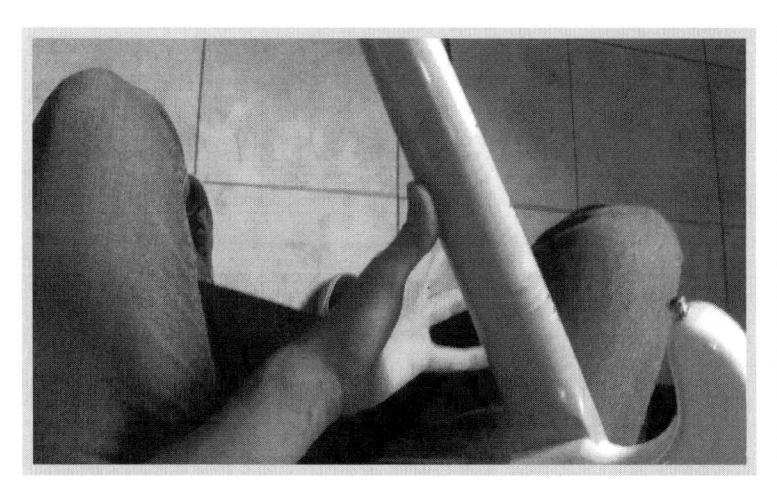

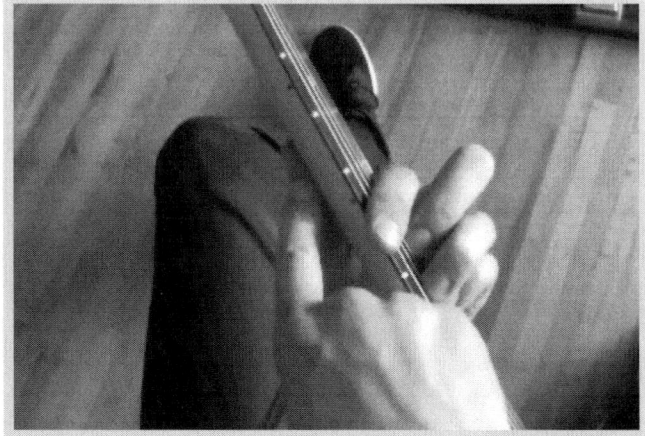

What you need to do is experiment with the placement of your thumb. I usually place the hardest part of my thumb (the opposite side of the knuckle) into the center part of the back of the neck. Try this out and move it around to find the position that works best for you.

Top 4 Tips To Play Crystal Clear Barre Chords For Life!

1. You gotta get that first finger hanging over the edge.
2. Find the best thumb placement for a good grip.
3. Make sure your wrist is in the 90* "Backwards dinosaur arm" position
4. Experiment and tweak your hand position and technique. These are guidelines to help you have a breakthrough of your own!

You've gotta experiment, OK? Now, I really have to be clear about this - there is no correct way to play barre chords. WHATEVER WORKS. Whatever gets the chord 100% crystal clear is the right way for you. These are guides that have been proven to work in my experience, so I hope they help you like they've helped my students!

Rather Connect By Phone? Call us:
1-855-974-7539

MAKE MONEY WITH YOUR GUITAR

Teach Beginners How To Play The Guitar

QUIT YOUR DAY JOB & MAKE UP TO $5,000 A MONTH
(While only working 20 hours a week)

Will Ripley's

GUITAR INSTRUCTOR ALLIANCE

Get access to a full, A-Z business building course that covers everything a new guitar instructor would need to know.

Discover how to get students, how to teach guitar & how to create a powerful, online presence that will ensure a steady stream of money…for doing what you love!

Sign Up For The "Guitar Instructor Blueprint" & Free Training Videos at:
WWW.WILLRIPLEY.COM/TEACHERSTOOLS

CHAPTER 28

MASTER 2 "E-STRING" BARE CHORD SHAPES

2 Barre Chord Shapes On Your E-String

Let's talk about the most common barre chord shape. You can play this anywhere, but let's use this diagram to help us play this chord on the first fret. To play this, you'd use your first finger to lay flat and hold down all the strings on one fret. It's like you've moved all of the notes of an E chord up a semitone! Check out this diagram. Can you see the 1st finger barre, plus your E major chord? Bonus points if you can see a power chord inside of this shape too!

Holding that barre with your first finger is going to allow you to play all the strings and all of your chords, **ALL** over the neck.

Take a look at the chord chart in the picture:

1. The thick bar on the top and no other markings tells us we're starting with the first finger on the first fret.
2. The bracket stretched between the "1's" tells us to hold down all of the

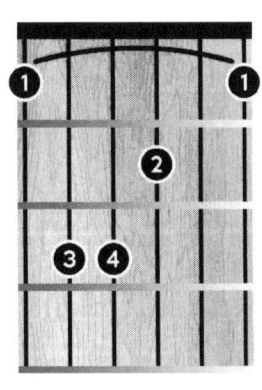

strings on the first fret.
3. It continues to read as normal with the second finger on the second fret and the third and fourth finger tucked up next to each other on the third fret.
4. This is essentially an E major chord moved up 1 fret - can you see the E major chord inside of the chord diagram?
5. There is a power chord inside of this barre chord - can you see that this barre chord is essentially an extension of a power chord?

Well, What Chord Is It?

This is your F major barre chord. "F" because that is the note you're playing on the first fret of the low E string. This is called your **"root note"**. It is the lowest sounding note compared to all the other notes on the other strings.

The chord is **major** because of its positive/happy sound when played. We're essentially just moving an E Major chord up 1 fret. Playing this chord shape on **any** fret will continue to give you that major sound.

How To Play ANY Major Chord Using This Shape

Let me use an example here. Go ahead and play this chord on the 3rd fret. Your root note is now a G, so you now have a G major barre chord!

Refer back to your notes on the fretboard chart if you need a refresher.

Continuing on, try to move that same shape up again to the 5th fret and you now have a A major barre chord!

You might be wondering...

I already know what a G Major and A Major chord are! We learned those already! Well, here's the special thing about barre chords, you're now able to take a chord and choose how you want it to sound.

Yes, a 5th fret major barre chord from the E-string is an A Major chord - this is true. An A Major chord can also be played in the open position like we've discovered in earlier chapters. So they are technically same, but as I'm sure you'd agree, they sound very different. What you may not know is that they can have different applications. We're going to get into this exciting new way of playing very soon… let's get back to that barre chord.

Let's Talk About Those Minor Chords

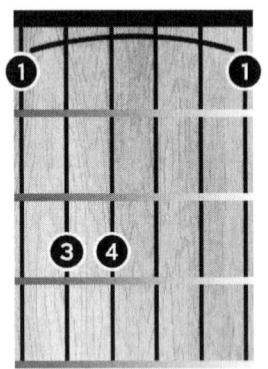

Here on the left is your F minor barre chord. In comparison to the major shape, it may seem easy to just remove your second finger, but be careful, if your first finger barre isn't holding down all those strings, it won't sound like a minor chord at all!

*The note that makes this barre chord minor is on that G string, so make sure it's sounding out.

Can you see the similarities with the E major and E minor chord structures? Barre chords just move this formation up one fret. The barre that the **nut** of the guitar provided when you play your open E is now replaced with your **finger.**

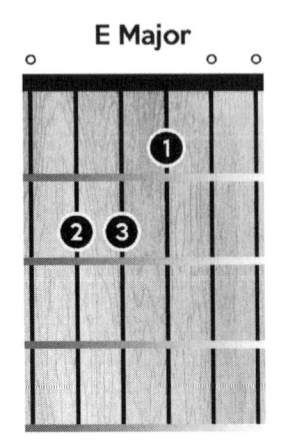

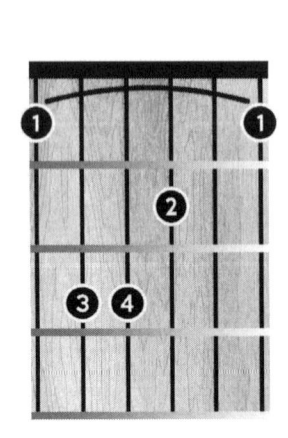

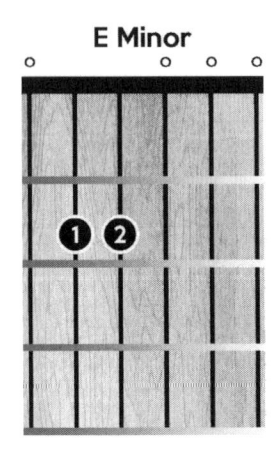

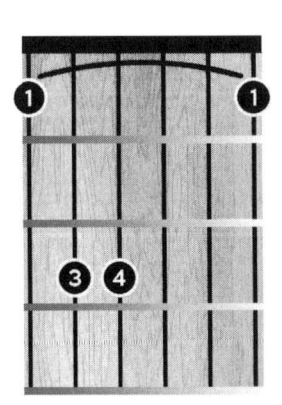

E Major

E Minor

115

To Sum Up Barre Chords On The E-String

- *Just like power chords, you can use these same formations all over the neck*
- *Within a bar chord, there is a power chord*
- *When looking at the diagram you should be able to see 2 things inside your E-string barre chords - #1 - Barre chords are just extensions of power chords and #2 They are just E major or E minor chords moved up*

CHAPTER 29

MASTER 2 "A-STRING" BARRE CHORD SHAPES

Barre Chords pt.2

We're going to *blast* through this chapter. These next 2 barre chords share the exact same concepts and approach. However, we will be using 2 fresh finger shapes, both of which are rooted from the A-string.

Quite simply, we're going to play what you know already - an A Major and A Minor chord in their 'open positions' and just **move them up 1 fret**. Boom! Same chordal structure, that gets a different finger shape and therefore, providing us with a new chord.

So, by playing your A major and your A minor chordal shapes up 1 fret with these new fingerings, you'll simply be playing an A# major chord and an A# Minor chord. This is because our **root note** is now on the 1st fret of the A string instead of our 'open A'.

*Because of those "enharmonics" that you learned about in the previous chapter on "notes on the fretboard", these could also be called Bb major chord and a Bb Minor chord.

These charts below show the **major and minor barre chord** shapes that are played when starting on the **A string**. Just like the major and minor shapes for the E string, these are simply a way to give the same chord, a different sound.

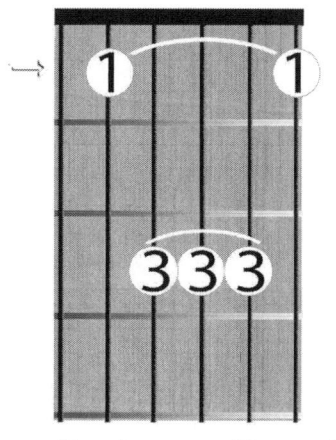

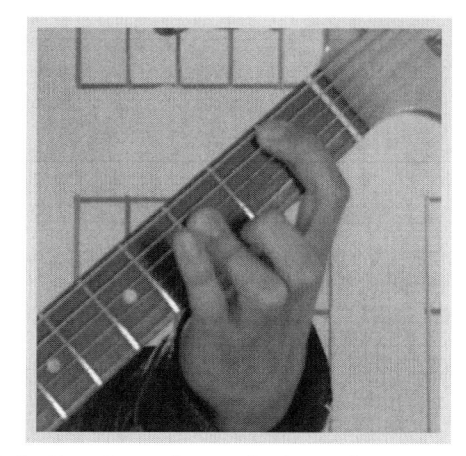

Don't worry if your high E string doesn't ring clear on this major shape. 4 notes is sufficient for this chordal shape!

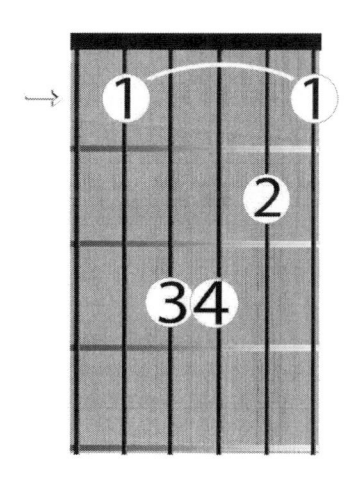

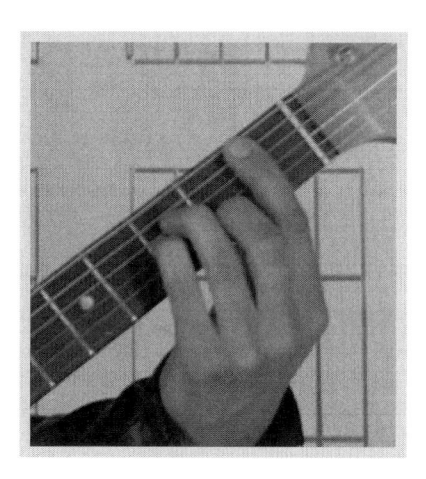

Very soon (if not already!), you'll be able to play **any** major and **any** minor chord starting from your A string using these shapes and your knowledge of the notes on the fretboard. See if you can find a D Major barre chord starting from your A-string and compare it to your D major open position chord. And hey, while you're at it - why not find a D major chord starting from your E-string major barre chord position!

Answer:
Play the A major barre chord shape from the 5th fret of the A string to get a D major.
Play the E-major barre chord shape from the 10th fret of the low E-string to get a D major.
Play the 'open position D major chord, you'd use that shape we've played a lot like in songs like "Sweet Child O' Mine" - (They are all the same chord!)

To Sum Up Barre Chords On The A-String

- On these A string rooted barre chords, you **do not** play the low E string.
- On the major shape, it's nearly impossible to let the high e-string ring with the 3rd finger barre - so honestly, don't worry about it! Just get 4 strings to ring clearly (the A, D, G, B strings). Additionally, you don't have to barre your first finger - only your 3rd finger.
- Some people find it best to mute the low E-string by touching it with the tip of their first finger while playing these A-string rooted barre chord shapes.
- There is a power chord inside of each barre chord shape. You can think of any of the 4 barre chord shapes as "extensions of power chords".
- You will find your A Major and A Minor chordal shapes inside of these A-string rooted barre chords.
- Barre just means using one finger to hold down strings.

CHAPTER 30

BARRE CHORDS MASTERY SONG LESSON "CREEP"

Barre Chords "Creep"

This is your barre chord graduation! We are going to be using barre chords, to learn Radiohead's "Creep" **in two different ways.** This song will help us explore how powerful this concept of playing the same chords in different voicings can really be!

Radiohead were attempting to record their debut album "Pablo Honey" but things didn't go well. They ended up releasing one song, recorded in one take, that wasn't really on the list. "Creep" was added to the album when it was released, one year later in 1993. The song was a huge hit for the band and they struggled to accept it's success. Thom Yorke, Radiohead's singer used the chord progression and a little bit of melody from the song "The Air That I Breathe" that was recorded by a band called "The Hollies" in 1973. It is yet another song that continues to get attention and has been covered by many famous artists around the world.

Reference the song or the video to get familiar with the progression. This song uses the same classic strum pattern as paradise city so you can really focus on gripping these barre chords.

First, we're going to learn the version of "Creep" that incorporates barre chords with their root note on the low E string. Start working on the chord charts below.

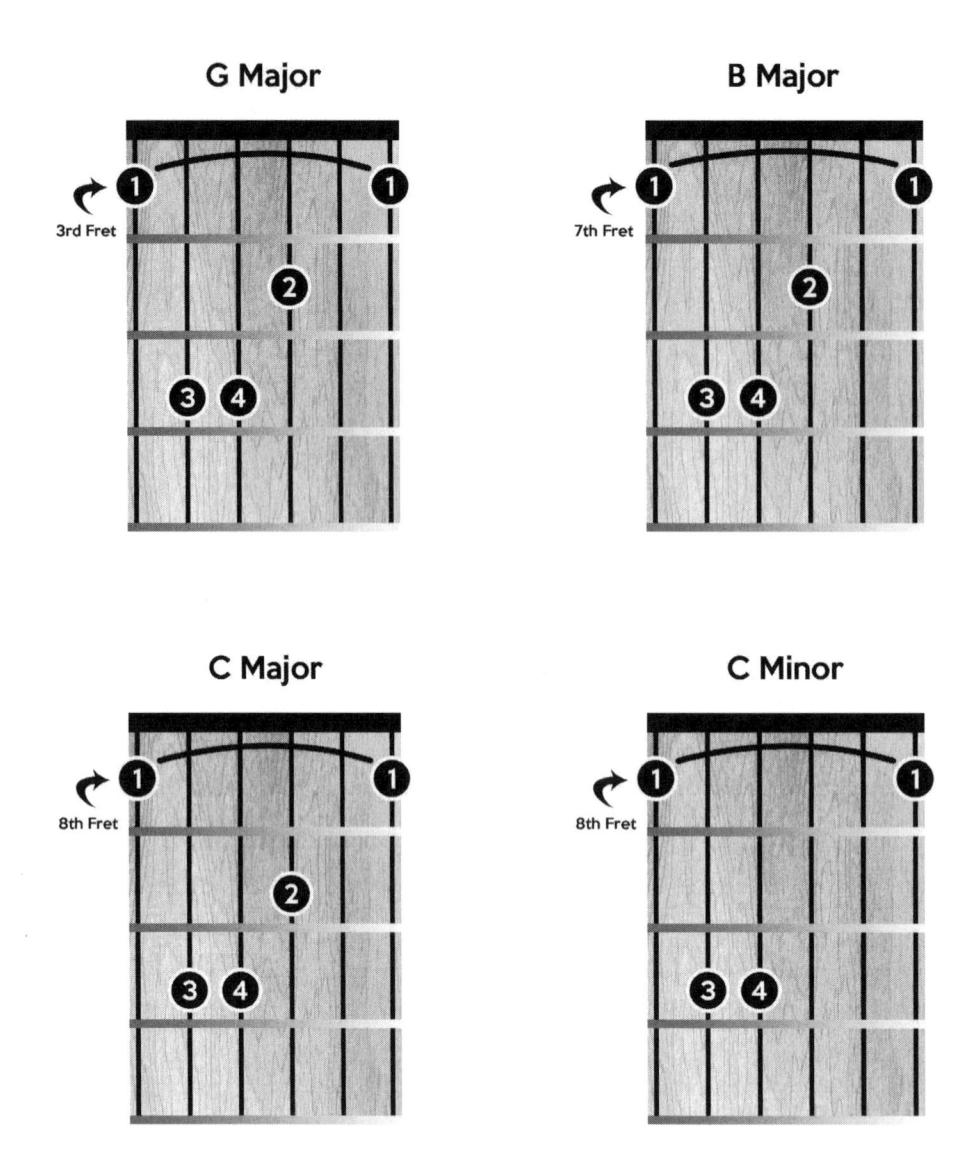

G Major
(3rd Fret)

B Major
(7th Fret)

C Major
(8th Fret)

C Minor
(8th Fret)

Because we're using full barre chords and starting on the low E string, try to get all of your strings sounding clear and ringing out, all the way up to your high e string.

We can play this same chord progression in a very different way. The alternate version of this song has all the same chords, but they will be in the form of barre chords that start on the A string. This will make them sound different, and a big part of that is to do with the fact that we **don't use our low E string** at all.

121

Your Barre Chord Mastery CHALLENGE

The next page will go through the alternate version. Before you go there, your challenge is to find all of these chords and play the exact same song from the A string. Do it without looking and you will be on your way to easily playing these barre chords all over the neck!

Follow these steps:

1. Find the G, B, and C root notes on the A string. Go back and reference the lesson "Notes on the Fretboard" if you need a refresher on how to find these notes.
2. Play the chord from the A string in the appropriate major or minor barre chord. Think about your A major or A minor chord shape moved up.
3. Lock this new progression in memory and add the strum pattern to complete the song.

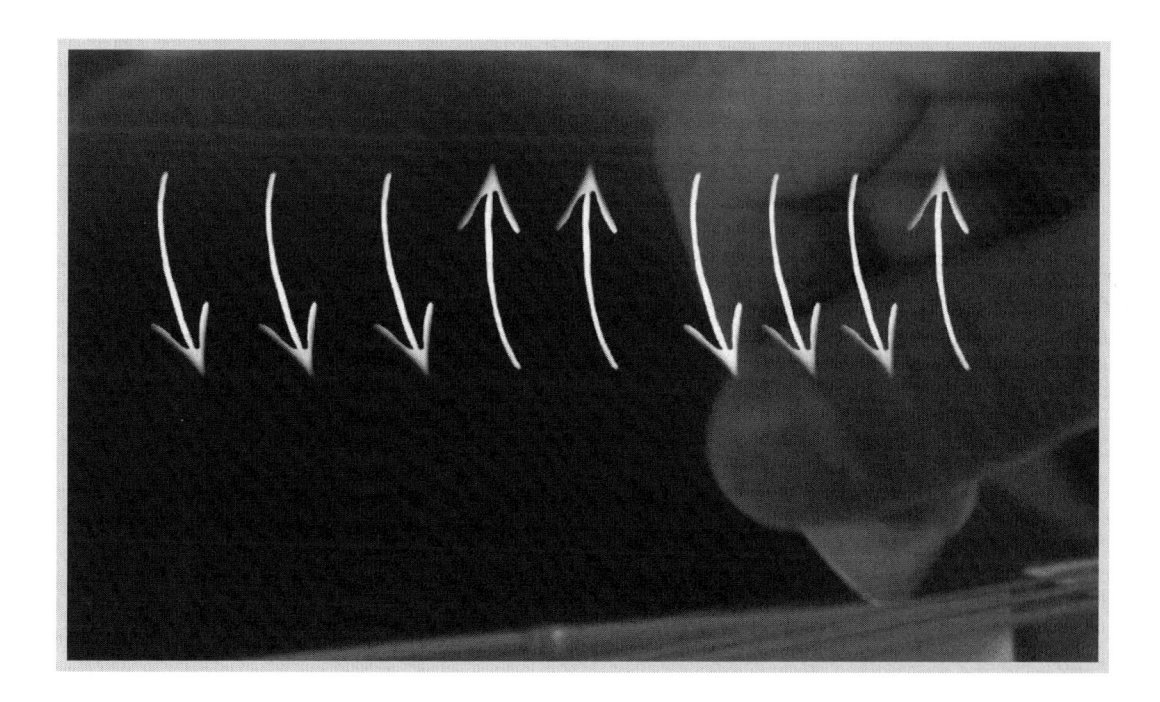

CHAPTER 31

PART 2: BARRE CHORDS MASTERY SONG LESSON

Creep Pt.2

Transposing the chords into a higher/lower register means taking the **same chord** and playing them **one octave up/down** on the guitar.

The first chord we learned for this song was a G. To transpose this chord up, you need to find the G note on your A string.

Quick tip: the 12th fret is the same note as the open string. Because the musical alphabet only goes from A to G, from the octave (or 12th fret) on your A string, go one whole step down (two frets down) to quickly find your G!

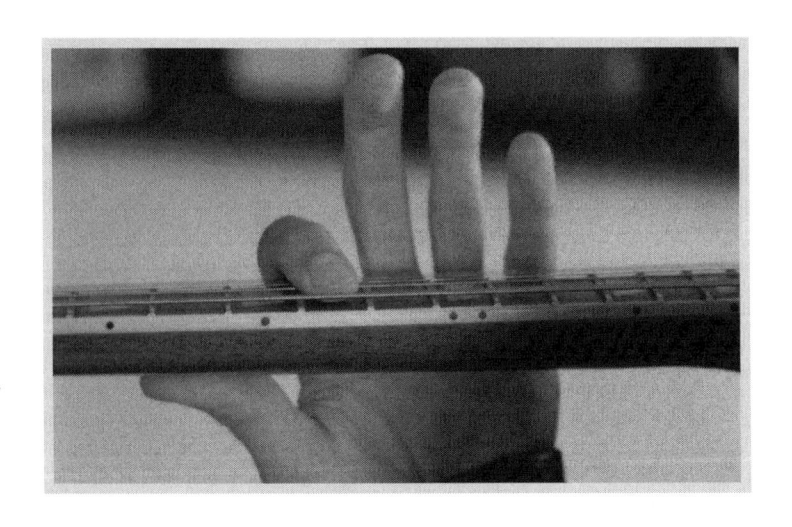

The last piece of the puzzle is choosing your major or minor barre chord formation. Then you've got all the chords! And if you followed the steps in the last chapter, you'll have 2 totally different ways of playing the chords that have a very different sound...but are technically the same chord. Look at you go, you guitar genius!

The next chord, B major is the same barre chord formation, found down on the 2nd fret.

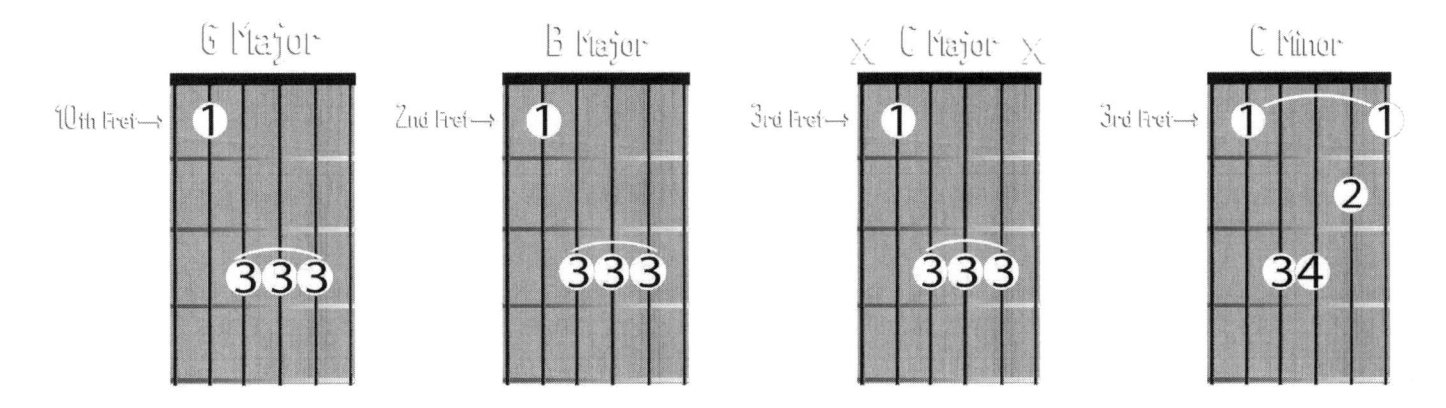

Then move everything up one fret, from B to C on the A string.

With the C minor, we stay on the same root note (3rd fret) and switch our finger formation to the minor barre chord shape.

Being able to play the same song or progression in a different way allows you to change the feeling of the same chord. This song gives us a great intro into how this works, it will prepare you to unlock the most unique chords, all over the neck.

The BIG Picture - Mastering Your Chords + Playing "Creep" For Practice

We just learnt 4 chords in 2 different ways, but they're the same chords… So, what's the deal?

Here's the big picture.

This song repeats the same 4 chords throughout the ENTIRE song. Yes, songs can be this simple. But take a listen to "Creep". The verse is so soft and chill and the chorus is huge and intense. Volume, intensity, and distortion levels help make the huge contrast between the verse and the chorus.

Now for YOU…

You are one person with one guitar. Chances are you don't have the rhythm section of

Radiohead sitting in the same room as you backing you up as you switch from the verse to the chorus.

What this means is that we need to try to encapsulate the drums, bass, and all that emotion and nail all the variations between the parts of the song all within one guitar and one person.

Long story short - try this…

Play the chords on the verse as your barre chords rooted from your A-string. Starting with that G major chord on the 10th fret. Strum lightly. You'll pretty much nail the vibe as one person with one guitar.

When the chorus comes up, switch to the barre chords rooted from your E-string. You'll get bassy, full sounding chords. Strum hard! You'll pretty much nail the intense energy as one person with one guitar.

So whether you love this song or just think it's so-so - it's a great exercise to learn your chords and access the variance of energy between the verse and the chorus. Since the chords stay the same throughout the verse and the chorus - we need to access different intensity and volume levels. By playing chords in different areas of the guitar we can simulate the "whole band" experience.

Keep on rippin' it up!

WE'RE ON A MISSION TO GET 2000 KIDS GUITAR LESSONS THIS YEAR

"Get Your Son Or Daughter Lessons From A Real Person, In Real Time, Without Having To Leave The House"

Kids are comfortable with technology! Now any kid with a computer and an internet connection can get music into their life in a big way

Go here and sign up for a FREE introductory session:
WWW.CAMPFIREGUITARSTAR.COM/KIDSCOACHING

Rather Connect By Phone? Call us. 1-855-974-7539

REFERENCE

THE PARTS OF A GUITAR

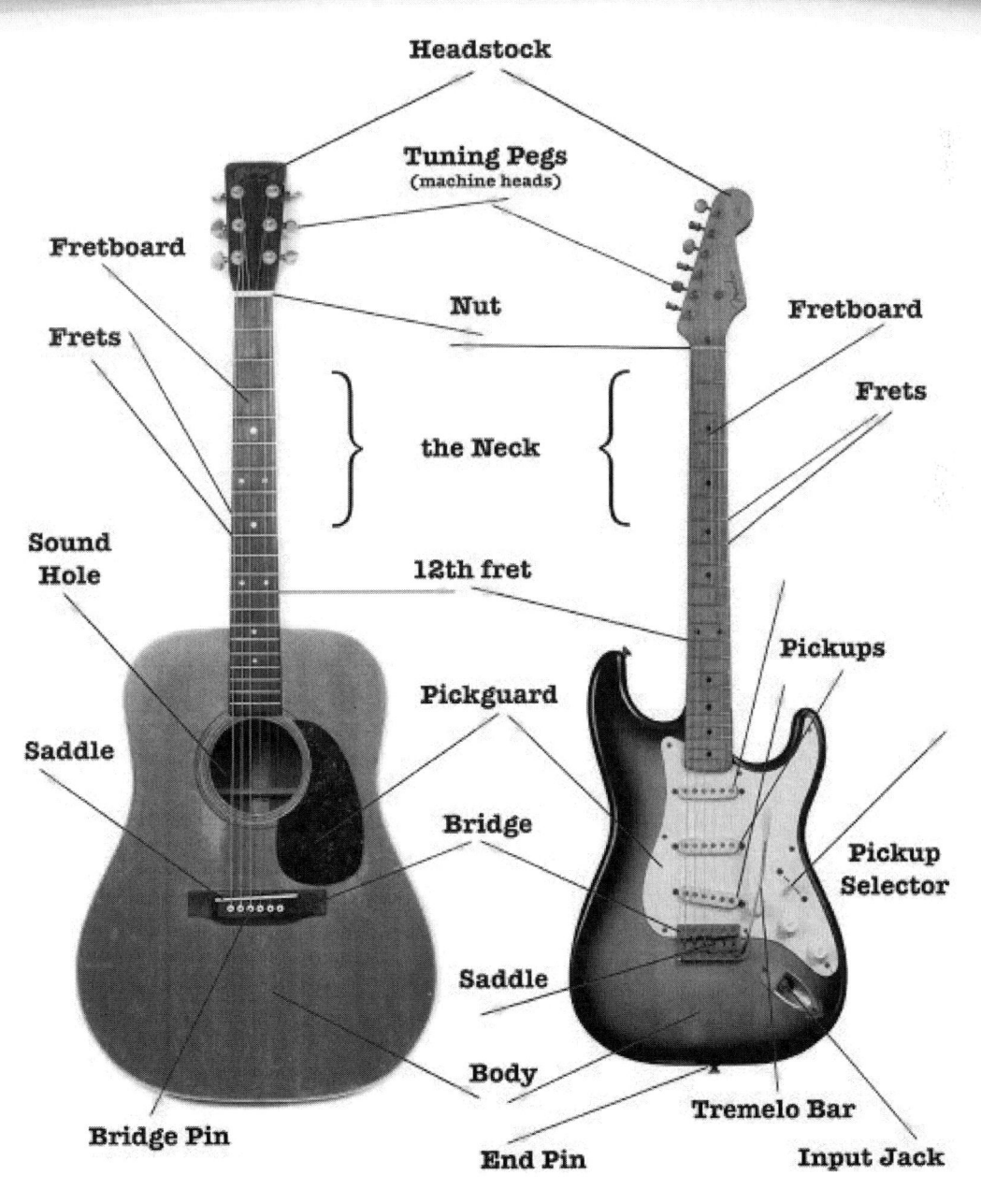

Labeled diagram of an acoustic guitar and an electric guitar:

- Headstock
- Tuning Pegs (machine heads)
- Fretboard
- Nut
- Frets
- the Neck
- Sound Hole
- 12th fret
- Pickguard
- Pickups
- Saddle
- Bridge
- Pickup Selector
- Saddle
- Body
- Bridge Pin
- End Pin
- Tremelo Bar
- Input Jack

CHORDS

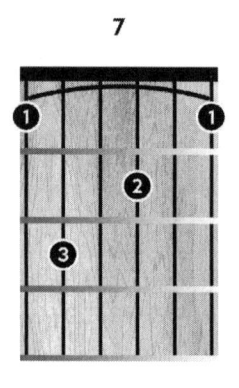

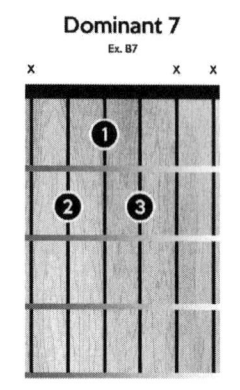

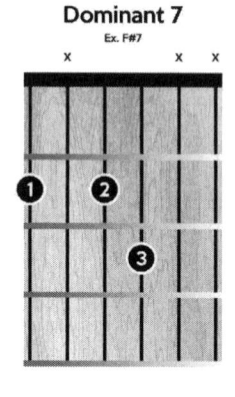

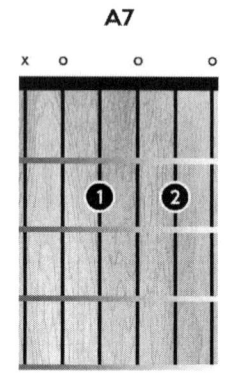

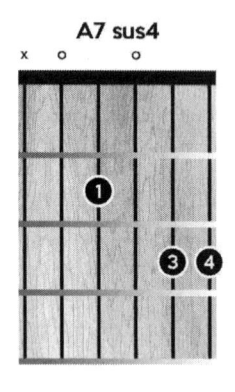

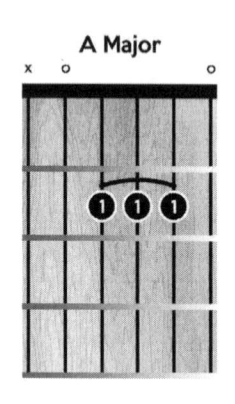

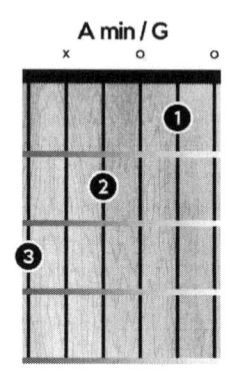

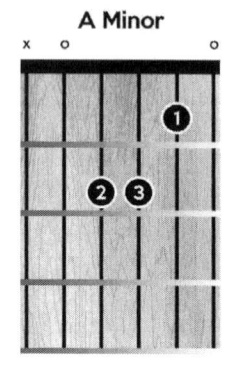

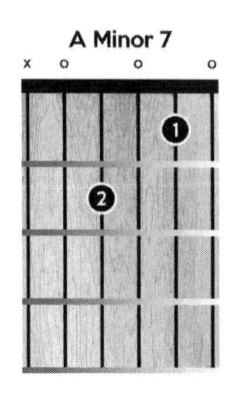

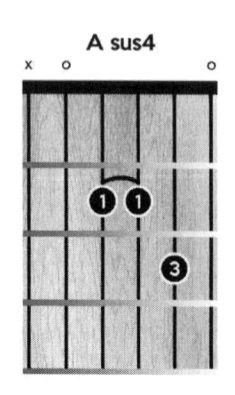

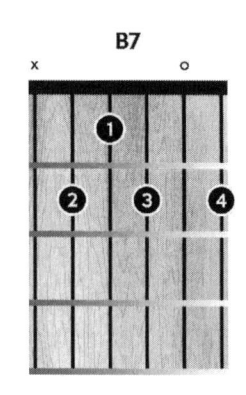

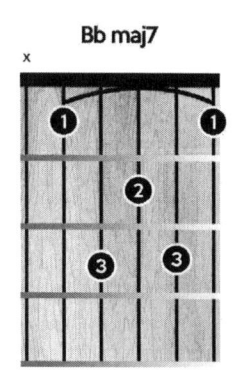

7	Dominant 7 Ex. B7	Dominant 7 Ex. F#7	A7

A7 sus4	A Major	A min / G	A Minor

A Minor 7	A sus4	B7	Bb maj7

130

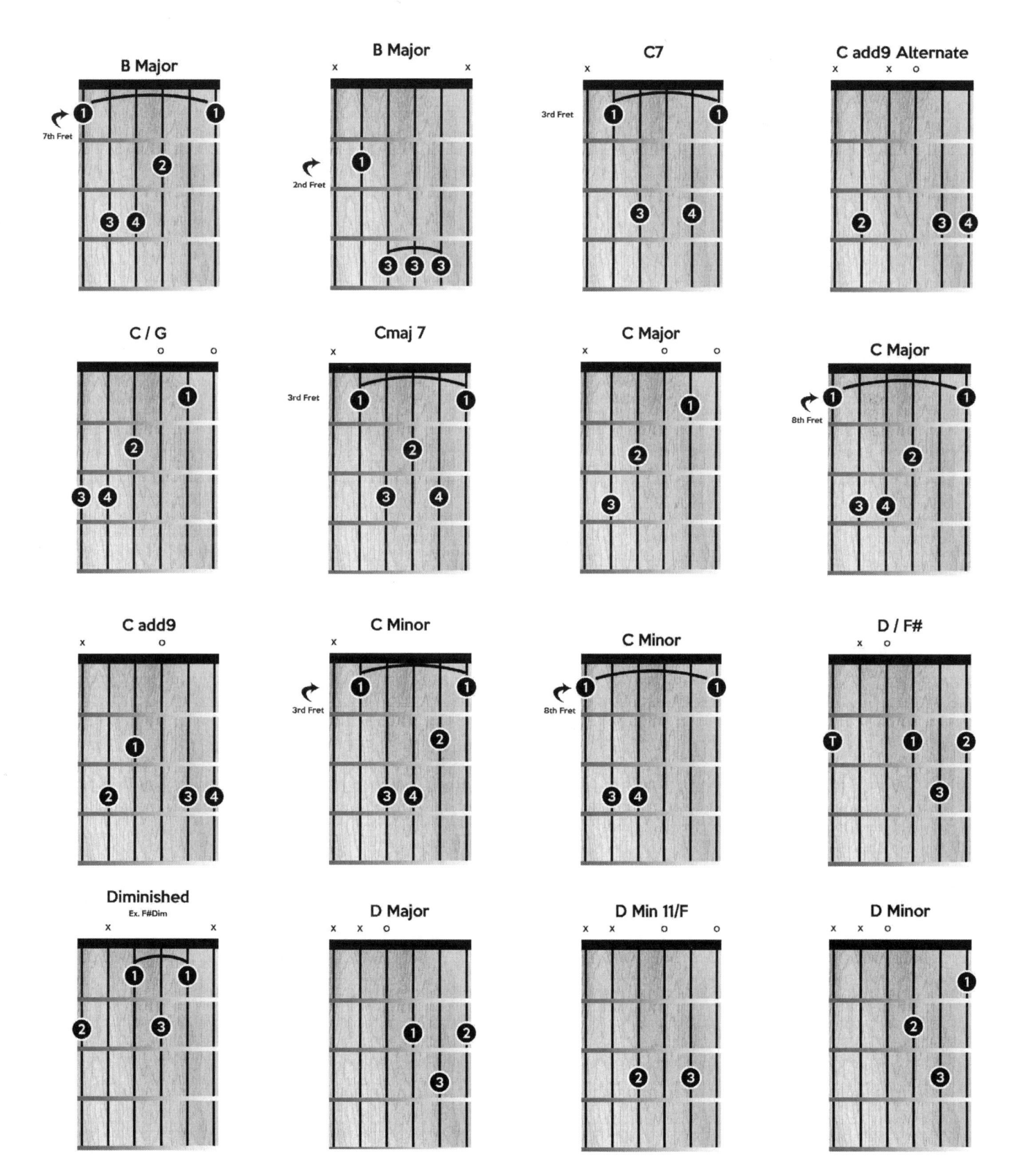

Dominant 7

Ex. C7

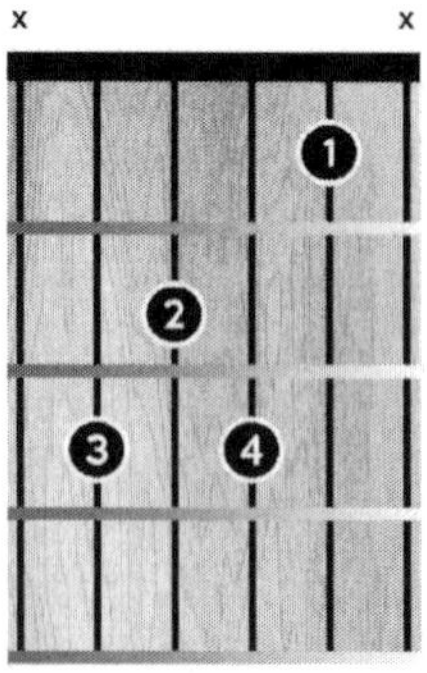

Dominant 7 #9

aka "Hendrix Chord"

Ex. B7#9

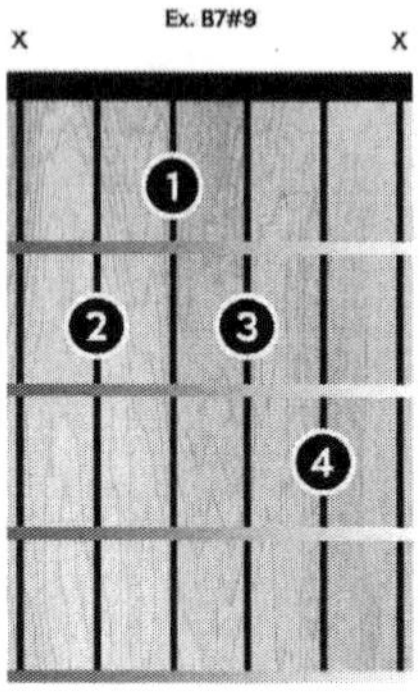

Dominant 7 add9

Ex: C9

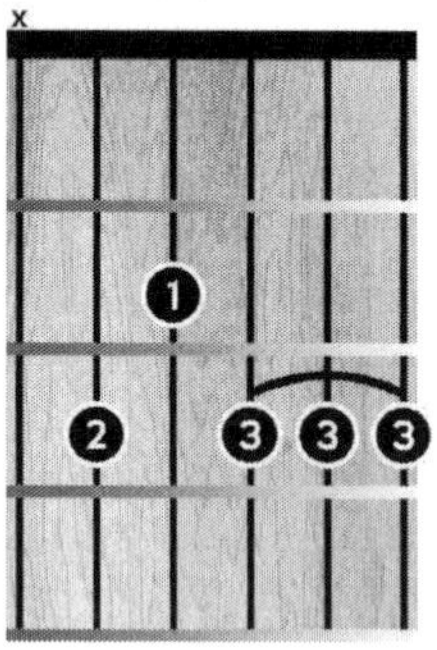

Dominant 7

Ex: Bb7

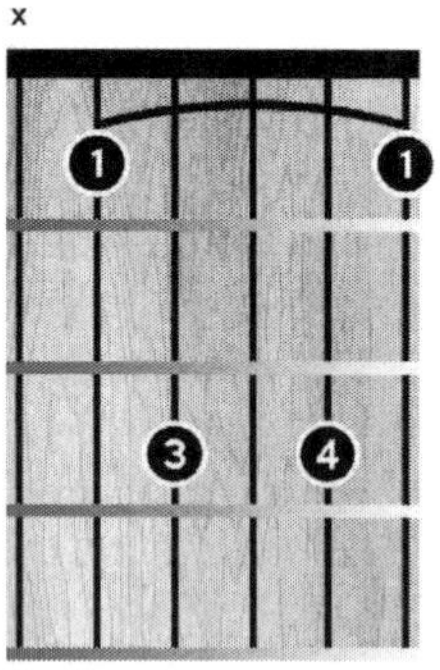

Dominant 7

Ex. F7

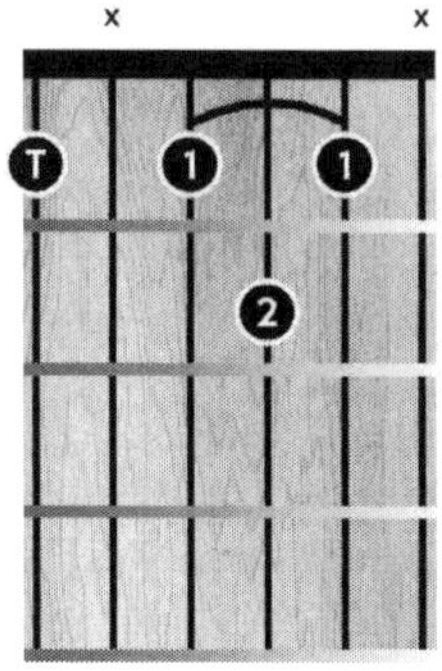

Dominant 7

Ex. F7

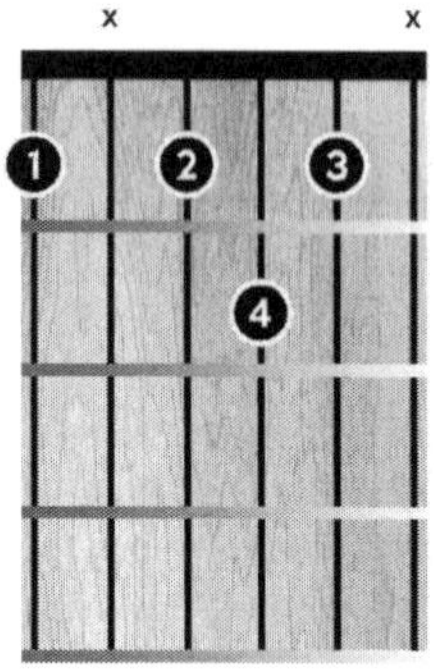

Dominant 7

Ex. F7

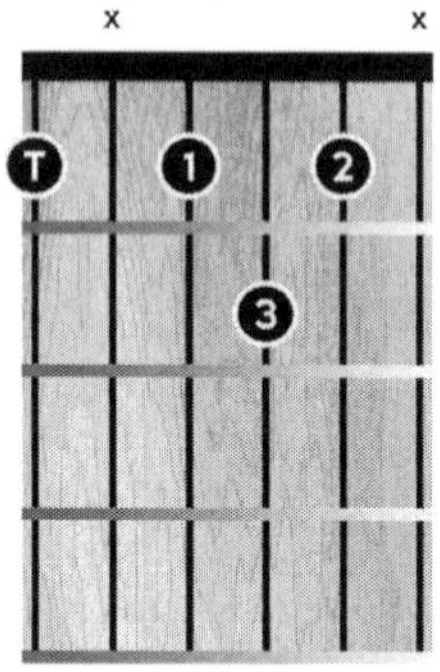

Dsus 2

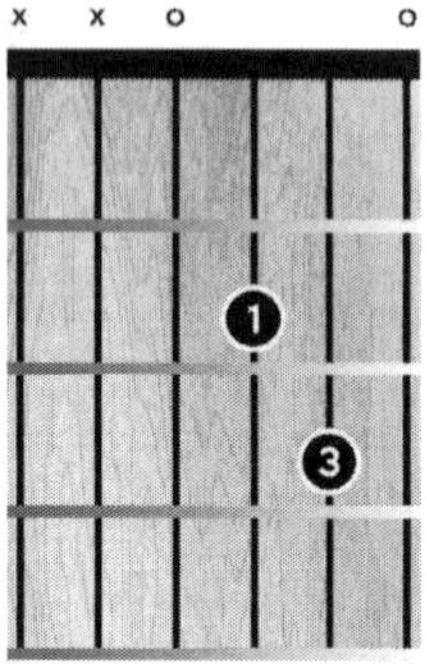

Dsus 4

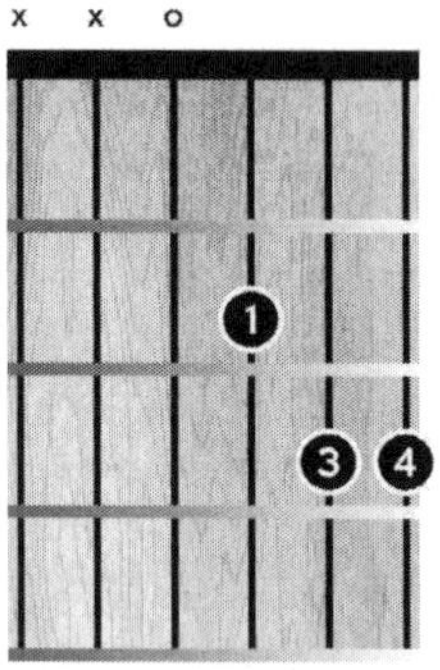

Dsus / F#

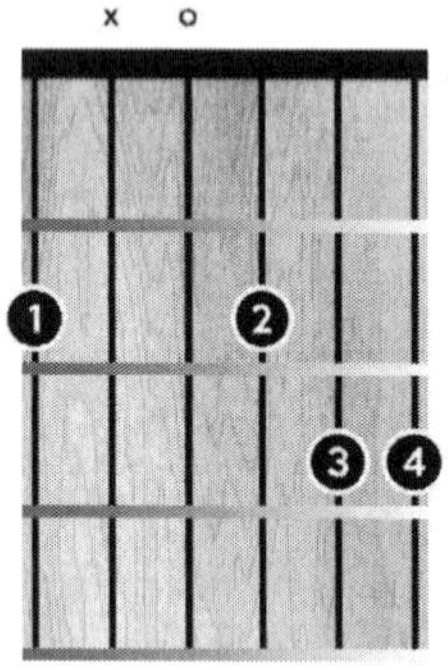

E

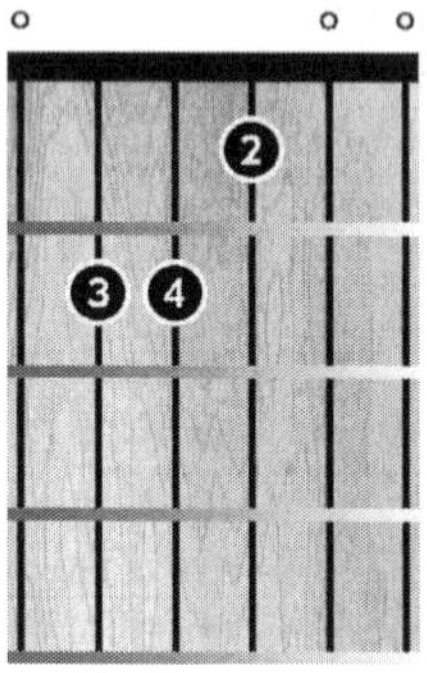

E7

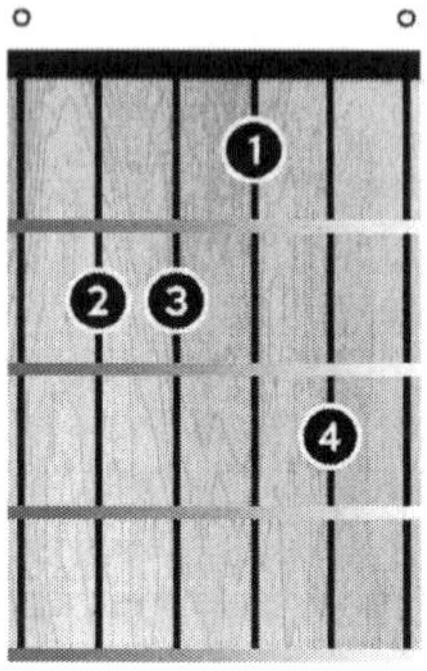

E7 b9

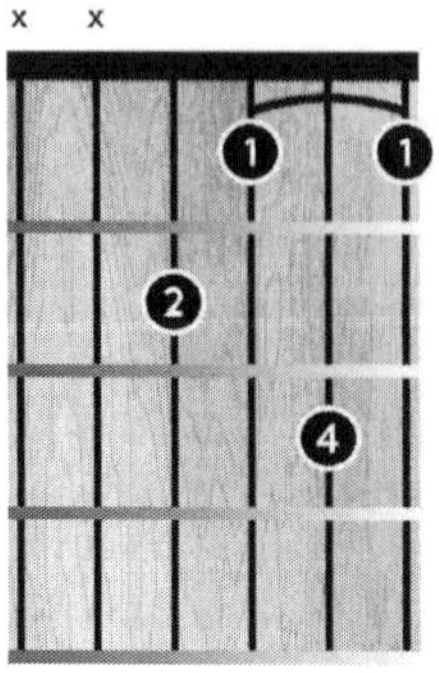

E7

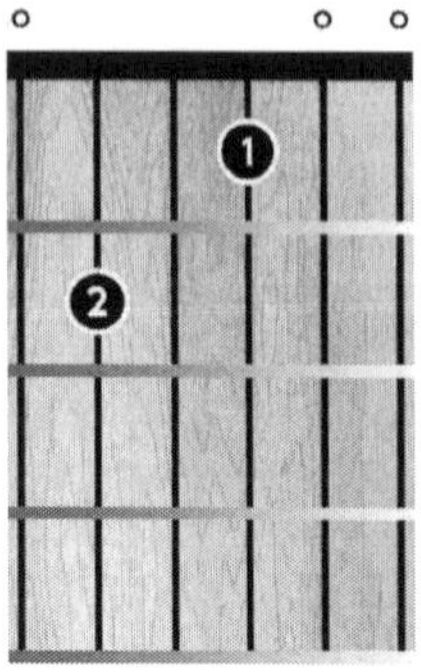

E Major

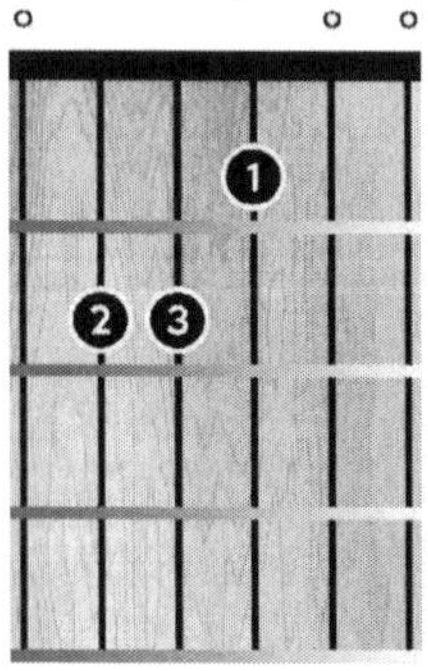

E Minor

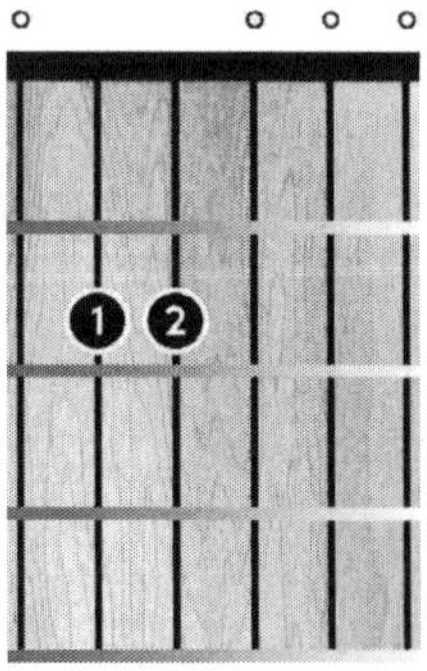

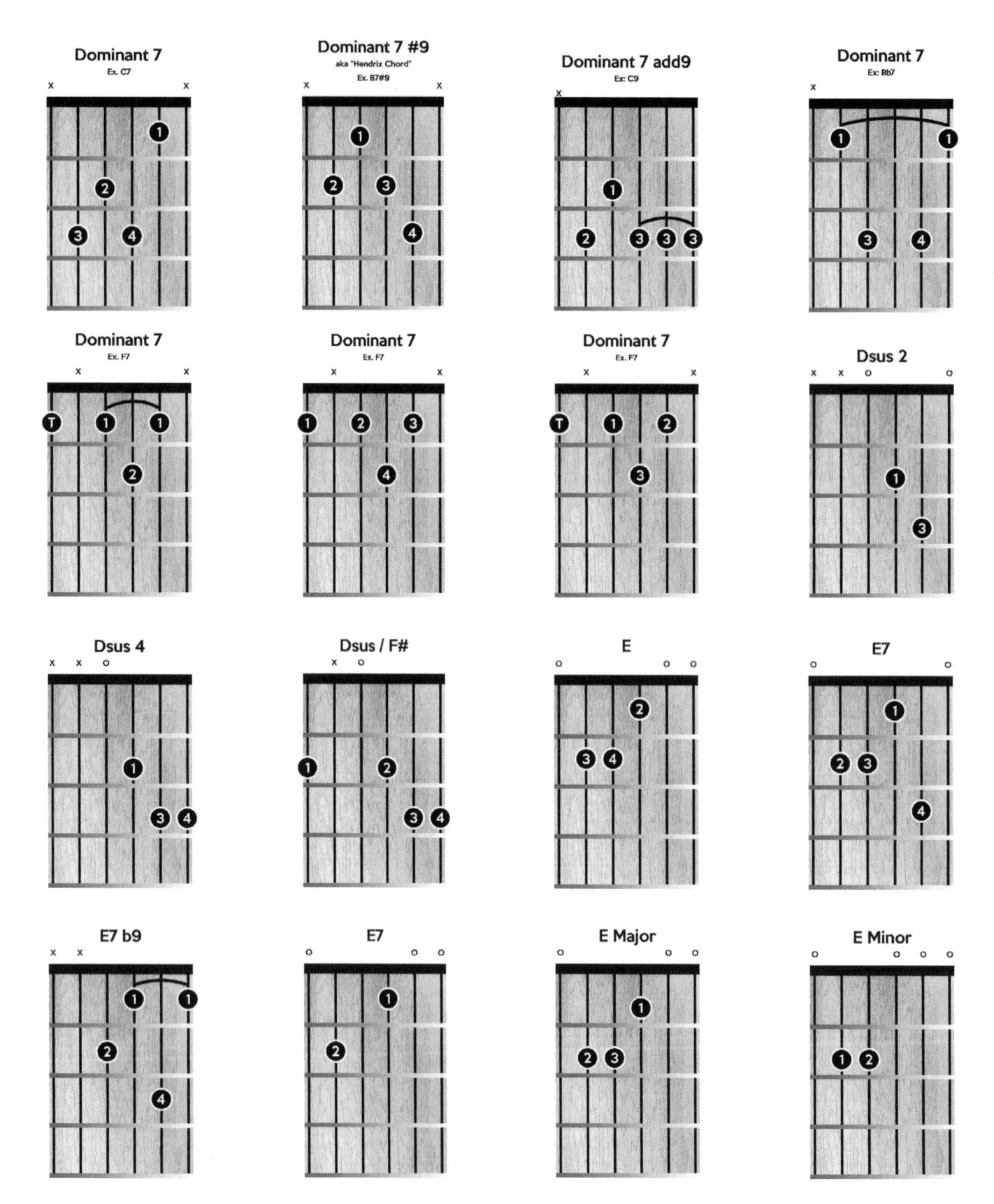

132

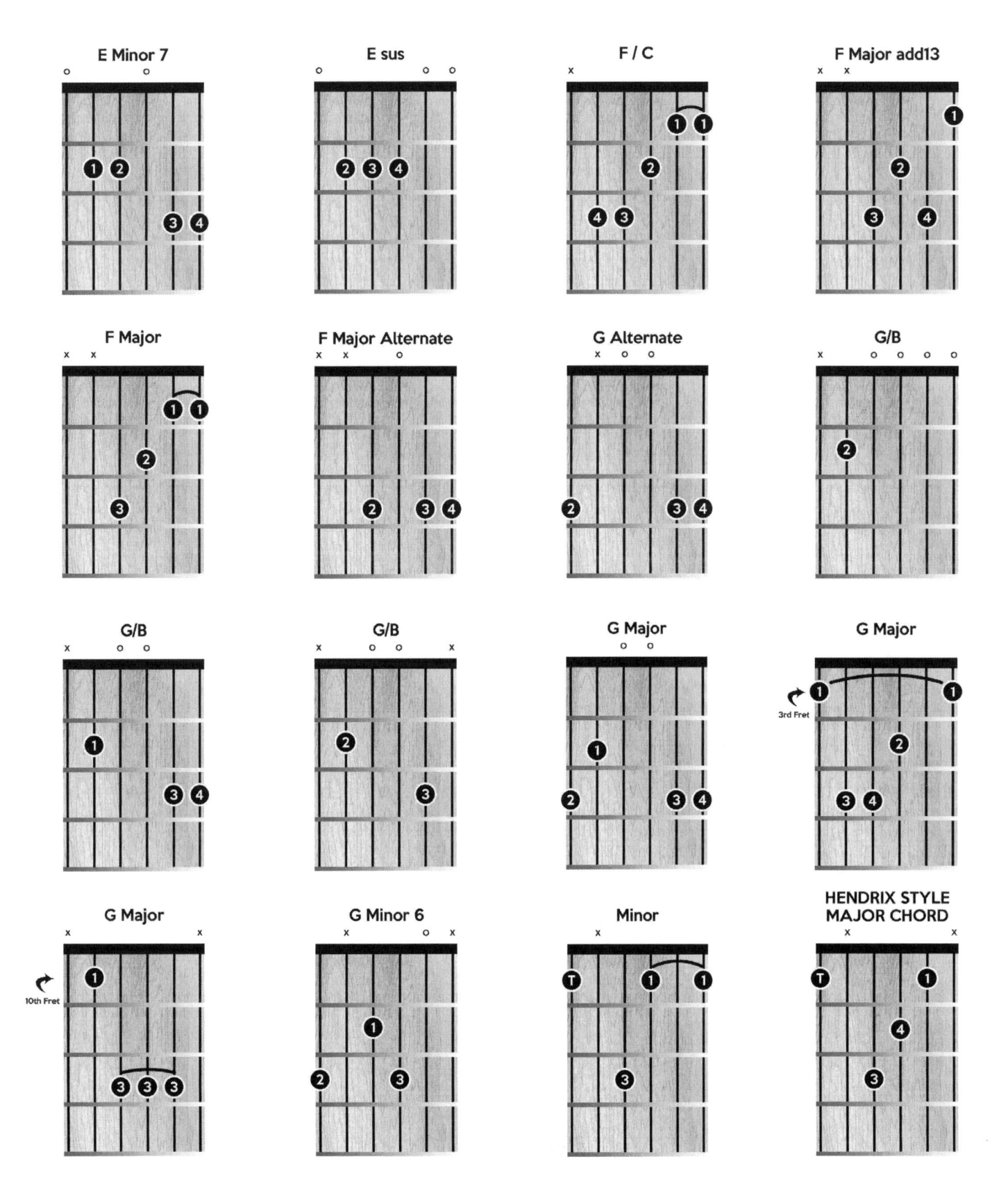

Chord Chart

HENDRIX STYLE MAJOR CHORD ADD9

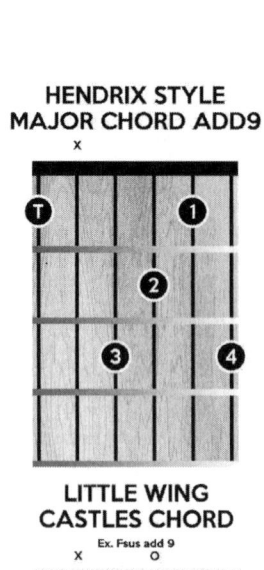

HENDRIX STYLE MAJOR CHORD ADD13
Ex. F maj 13

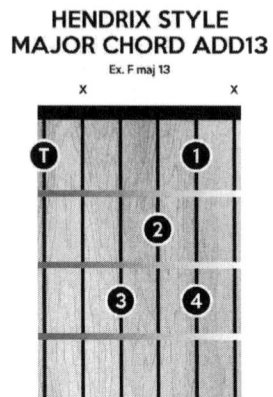

HENDRIX STYLE MAJOR CHORD
Ex. F major

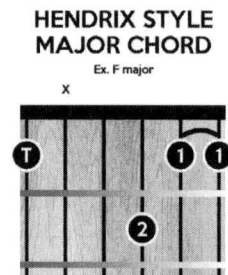

HENDRIX STYLE MAJOR CHORD
Ex. F major

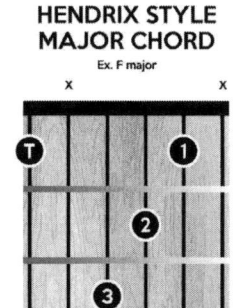

LITTLE WING CASTLES CHORD
Ex. Fsus add 9

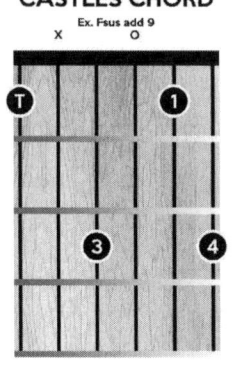

Major Barre Chord
Ex. F Major

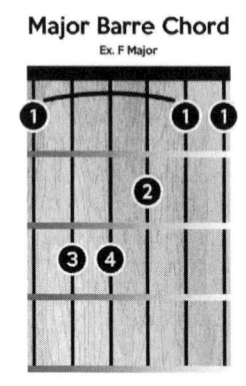

Major Barre Chord
Ex. F Major

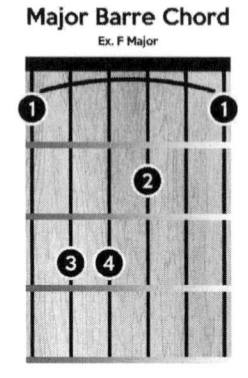

Minor 7

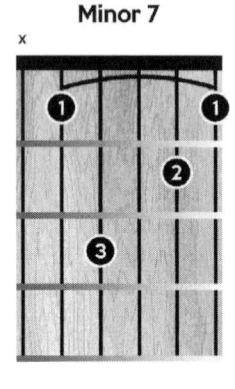

Minor 7

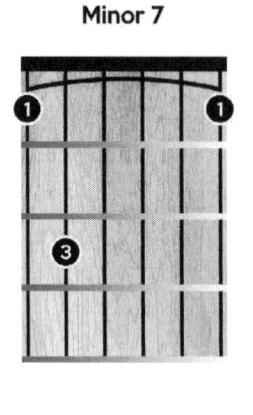

Minor Barre Chord
Ex. F Minor

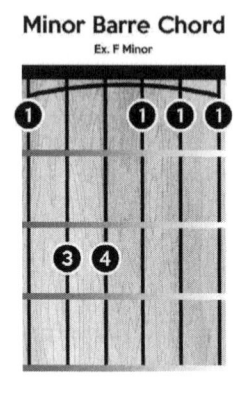

Minor Barre Chord
Ex. F Minor

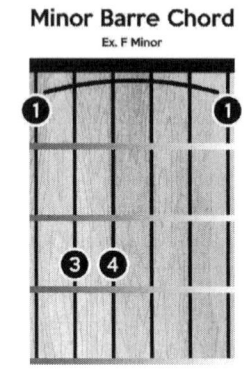

POWER CHORD #1

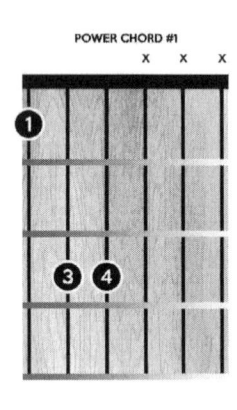

POWER CHORD #2

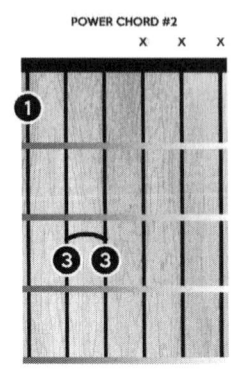

POWER CHORD #3

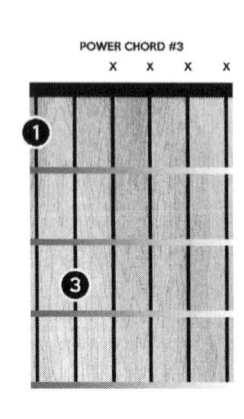

POWER CHORD #4

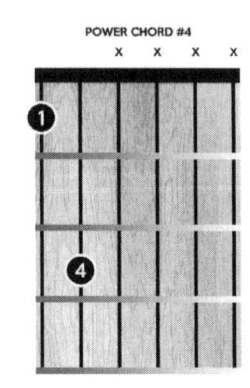

CHANGING YOUR STRINGS

Restringing An Electric Guitar & An Acoustic Guitar

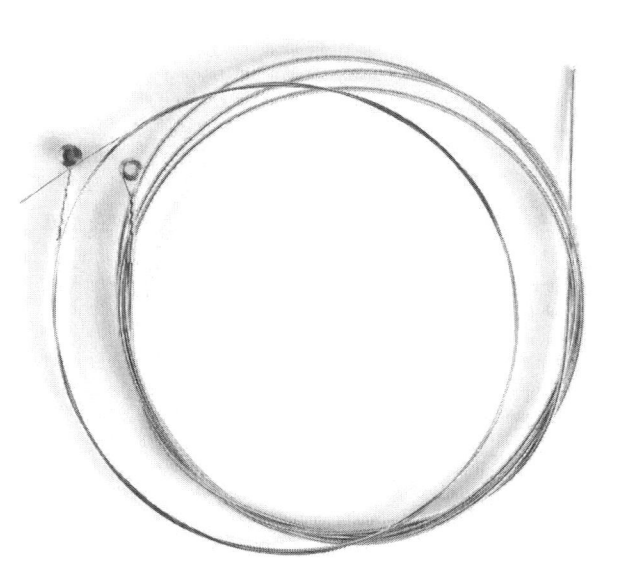

Kind of important? YES! Whether you're replacing one that broke or changing old dull set, fresh strings are the greatest thing on a guitar. They are a cheap and sure way to improve your instruments tone.

How do you know when to change your strings? Well, they should be shiny and metallic looking. Compare your old strings to your new strings. If they are obviously different in colour, that's usually a good sign! Also, if you're having problems with your guitar staying in tune, or if you're just looking to **improve the way your guitar sounds,** then look no further!

First things first; Get those old nasty strings off of the guitar. But wait! Don't snip them off when they're at full tension. Flexed wood doesn't like that too much. Loosen all the strings so there completely saggy and use whatever means necessary to get them off. Snip them with wire cutters or whatever. Just take them all off and put them in the garbage or some kind of metal recycling system you may have implemented. **Some People** believe that you shouldn't entirely relieve the guitar's neck of it's strings tension and will remove one string and replace one string at a time. This takes a bit longer, and I haven't had any problems with the steps that I have for you here in all the years of changing strings on my 8 guitars that I own (most are $2000 +).

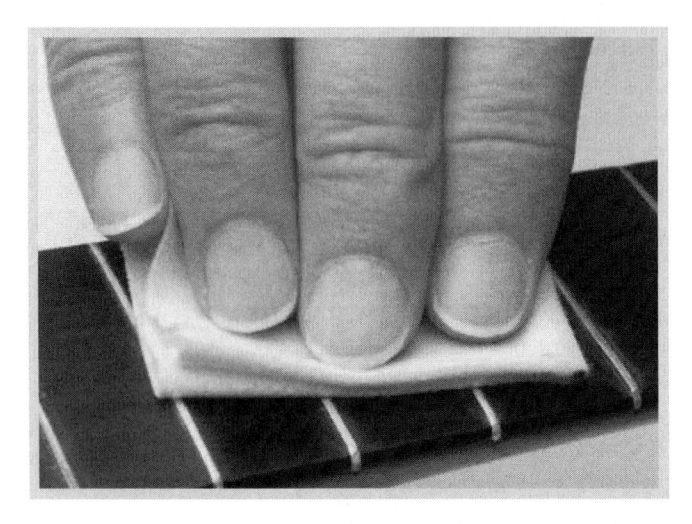

Now this is the time to give your fret board a **wipe down.** Using a clean, dry cloth, wipe down your fretboard to get rid of the dirt and oils that can accumulate. Make sure to dig around each side of the frets, as this is an area prone to buildup.

THE ONLY DIFFERENCES BETWEEN THE 2 STYLES OF GUITARS

For Electric Guitars

You just have to ask yourself one question…and it's not - 'Do I feel lucky?'….It's - **Do I have a Fender style Bridge or a Gibson style bridge?**

At the end of the day, we're just tightening strings around a post but these different style bridges are can certainly send us for a loop. A sure way to tell is: Do you insert the strings through the backside of the guitar and the strings actually go through the guitar's body? If yes, this is a Fender style bridge, commonly used on Strats and Tele's. So you'll probably have to take that white rectangular piece of plastic off the back (and some people leave them off). Basically, if you don't have this kind of setup, you have a Gibson style bridge, which is more self-explanatory.

For Acoustic Guitars

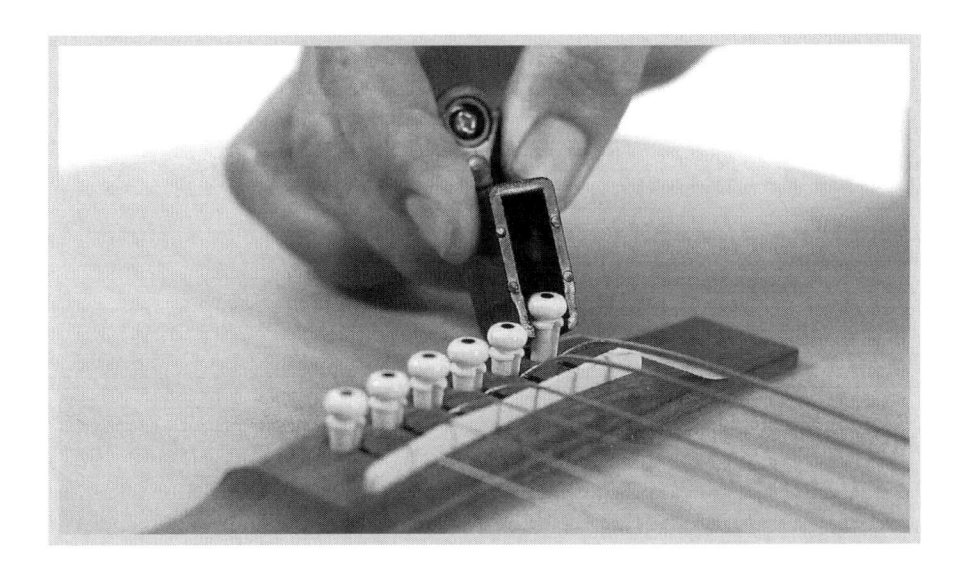

The only difference with acoustic guitars are those little pegs that hold the strings into the bridge - also called bridge pins. With the strings loosened off, try pushing the string into the bridge while pulling on the pin. If you can't get the pins out to release the strings from the guitar, reach your hand inside of the guitar, find the string pegs and push upwards on them so they pop out. Another is to use a set of pliers and pull them up and out. **The most convenient way** is to use a string winder tool. They all have a little area on them designed exactly for this purpose! Just insert the cutout area into the string peg, and pull up to pop them out of the body. Similar to using pliers, but it won't chew up your string pegs.

Put the string ball into the hole, insert the string peg with it's notch in the forward position so the notch points in the direction the string would go up the neck. **We want to get this string tightly** in there so it doesn't move when we start tightening the string - so grab the loose string and simultaneously pull on it, while holding the peg into place by pressing down on it. You'll feel it snug into place, you can even tug on it a bit to do so. Once it doesn't shift any more, that string is ready to be tightened up to pitch!

*Sometimes a peg might fly out or pop up while you're tightening the string. No worries, just loosen off the string a bit, makes sure everything is back in place and hold the peg down while tightening the string.

On an electric, simply feed the strings in order through the bridge of the guitar until it's held by the ball on the end.

The Saddle *(The thing you don't have to deal with)*

Reference "Parts Of The Guitar" to easily identify the saddle. On acoustics it is usually a removable strip of bone like composite. They are specially shaped to give your strings the right height, angle and to keep them in-tune as you play higher up the neck. If it falls out, place it back with the flat end into the body of the guitar and the curved edge facing up with the taller side under the lower strings.

On an electric guitar, your saddle is comprised of moving parts. The fine adjustments of height and length will allow your strings to sit in a good relation to each other and are a big determining factor to your guitar playing in-tune as you play up the neck.

If you feel like your strings are too high or go out of tune when you play notes past the 12th fret, you will have to have your guitar looked at by an experienced Luthier. Although it's not always the case, fine tuning the saddles will be part of the solution.

When we move on after this paragraph, the remaining points are the same whether you're re-stringing an acoustic or electric guitar! Woot!

So, let's get those new strings on, shall we?

Before you take the guitar strings out of the package, you should know they come in a specific order and they come organized in the box so you don't have to guess where the .036

size string goes and nonsense like that. If you jumped the gun on this and strings are out of the package and dangling everywhere, looks like you'll be using your eye to gauge which string goes where! **Lesson learned!** (strings almost always come out of the box in order).

Now that you have your fresh strings in the same order they came out of the box, guide each one into the bridge and move on until you have all 6 strings dangling from the bridge system.

*I like to do each stage to all 6 strings at the same time. The first stage would be putting all the strings through the bridge (electric) or put them all in the string pegs (acoustic) so all you have to do is grab individual strings and wind them up.

Now, let's wind 'em up! This is a finicky area and you will get some different opinions on this. I personally use extremely thick gauge strings so the idea of winding up my size 60 string to the tension of an E note is a little bit hard on the neck of the guitar, so it's a good idea for me to **evenly disperse the tension** of the strings.

So, how about we tighten the strings in this order: D, E, B, G, A, e

But wait! Before you do that there is **The most important thing ever that you must remember.** We NEED to have several string wraps around those winding posts! Why? Well, this helps keep the guitar in tune. If you can imagine, the more wraps you have, the more solid the connection the string has to the guitar so we run a very minimal chance of string slippage.

Before you tighten the strings, you need to have a certain amount of slack for each string to allow 2-3 wraps around the string post. **Your middle finger is good for a few things,** including a measuring stick for this purpose. With the string through the winding post, place the tip of your middle finger in the middle of the fret board (about 10th fret) and pull the string out of the winding post until it's reached the other end of your middle finger. This is roughly about how much slack you need on the string before you start winding. **Make sure your strings are winding around the tuning peg on the side closest to the middle of the headstock… And wind away!**

*To ensure nice clean wraps, you can guide the string using your hand while your other hand is winding the tuner with that handy string winder you bought!

So how much do you tighten the strings? First, just get them all tightened to the point where they're making a clear sound, or even a bit tighter than that. Stop tightening once the strings are all sustaining an audible tone. **Use your handy dandy electronic tuner** (you can download the Will Ripley tuner by searching "Will Ripley" in the App Store!) to tighten each string up to pitch. Don't over tighten and snap a string!

Wow! What a fiasco, **you're done! But not quite..** These are brand new steel strings that have never been put at this tension before. **They need help to stretch out!**

You can help this process by pulling up on each string at the 12th fret. Sometimes you'll actually feel the strings get looser as you pull on them! Now retune your guitar and repeat this process until the strings have relaxed and are holding their pitch.

I hope you found this article helpful. After going through this process many times, it will become second nature and something you might even enjoy doing because you know the rewards you hear with a fresh set of strings. So when your strings become discolored, don't sound as good as they used to and get buildup on them – It's time for a change!

TIPS ON BUYING A GUITAR
FOR A BEGINNER

There are positives to both starting on **acoustic** AND **electric**. Let's take a look.

STARTING ON A CLASSICAL ACOUSTIC

I would recommend a classical acoustic guitar for mostly everyone, but especially kids and teens. These have NYLON strings, not steel strings so they are a lot softer on the fingers. Play on one of these for a couple of months, then decide if you want to stay acoustic or go electric and take the plunge. Maybe while playing the classical guitar you'll find a new love for flamenco guitar! who knows...

STARTING ON ACOUSTIC (STEEL STRING)

Probably the biggest advantage of starting on an Acoustic is that it's hassle free. No amps, or cables or electronics to hold you back from focusing on the most important thing - playing the thing! It's nice to be able to head over to a friends house, down to a park or beach with just a guitar and a bag. Chances are, you're gonna buy an acoustic sooner or later! That's just what us guitarists do! (I have 4!).

An acoustic guitar just sounds so good. To get that sound, they are setup with thicker strings that are a bit rougher and tougher on the tips of your fingers. Are you asking: "So what's good about this?!" Well, you can ask any of my online or in-person students, I always say: "We gotta take our fingers to the gym!". Guitar isn't for the faint of heart. Especially any music that get's a harder edge. Playing acoustic just makes your fingers a bit tougher!

STARTING ON ELECTRIC

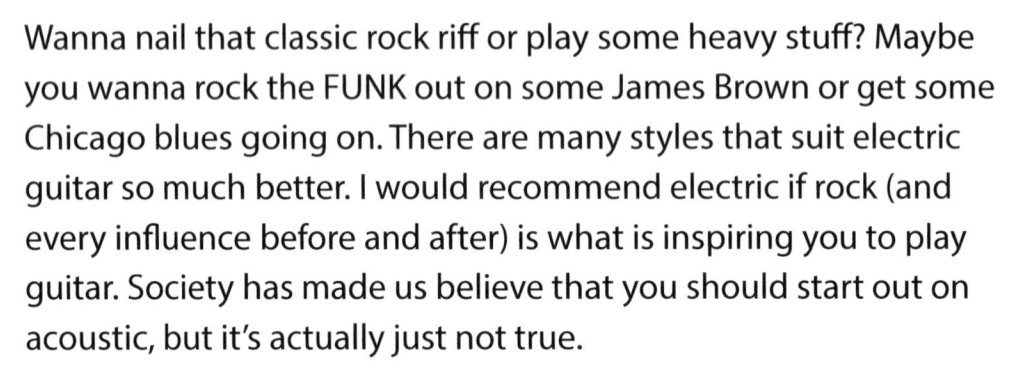

Wanna nail that classic rock riff or play some heavy stuff? Maybe you wanna rock the FUNK out on some James Brown or get some Chicago blues going on. There are many styles that suit electric guitar so much better. I would recommend electric if rock (and every influence before and after) is what is inspiring you to play guitar. Society has made us believe that you should start out on acoustic, but it's actually just not true.

Electrics are actually a bit easier to play because of their smaller body and neck. They are generally set up with strings that are up to 2 full sizes SMALLER than acoustic too! What this means is they are smoother, more bendy and easier to press down and thus, less taxing on the fingers. That sounds pretty appealing, doesn't it?

Versatility. If I were allowed only one guitar, I would pick the electric… it would have to have an amp that could have clean and dirty sounds. This way I could have my clean jangle jangle and then with a push of a switch I could rock out!

HOW MUCH SHOULD I SPEND?

Honestly? You want the real answer? As much as you can afford. Also, get something made in Japan, Canada, or the U.S if it fits your budget.

Brand name guitars (especially ones that are 10 years old and older) hold their value very strongly. If you can invest $1,500 in a 10 year old Gibson and decide you hate guitar...chances are, you can sell it without taking any hit on the wallet and regain your entire investment.

Expensive guitars are easier to play (first and foremost) and sound better. I should note again here that whatever guitar you have, I would highly recommend watching the first chapter on "playing a suitable guitar."

So! You've made your decision and it's time to get into checking out some guitars! **Let's get into the main points.**

CHECKING OUT A GUITAR

Basically, we want to make the **guitar as easy as possible** on ourselves, right? I mean, every guitarists favourite instrument will be the one that feels the best in their hands! The tips that I provide in this article will steer you in just that direction - making the beginner curve as smooth as possible.

There are 2 main things to look for. 1) The action 2) Buzzy notes

1) Everyone wants action, right? Well Guitar action refers to something a little bit different.

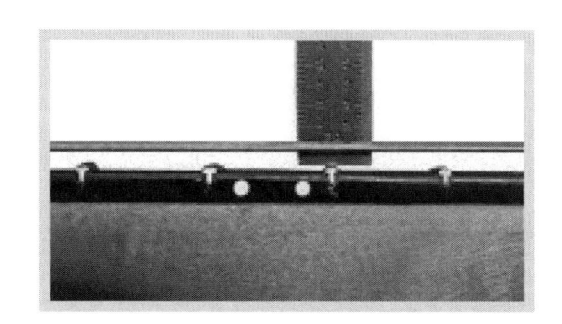

Action refers to *The height of the strings off of the guitar neck*. This picture shows a guitar with very *high* action. So, big deal? But the higher the strings are off

the fretboard, the further your fingers have to press the strings down to make a sound! Now generally speaking the closer the strings are, the better. If they get *TOO* close, we'll get **Buzzy Notes** which we'll get into in a moment.

Holding a guitar in your lap **in the playing position** you can get a good view of the strings and the height of them off the frets.

"The Eyeball Test"...

Look down at the very first fret (1st metal slot at the top of the neck) and take note of how high the string is off of the fretboard. Now, follow the string up the neck with your eyes. How much does the string change in height? If it drastically changes then this guitar needs some work done to it! What you want to see is *Roughly* a consistent string height off the frets ALL the way up the neck.

Now keep in mind, a slight change in height off the frets isn't the end of the world, in fact it's quite normal but we are looking for a certain level of consistency. The goal here is to have the string close to the frets.

2) Buzzy notes sound like garbage. They'll make a 2,500.00 Martin sound like a trash can! Buzzy notes are usually caused by strings being too low on the frets and will **buzz** against the other frets.

It helps if you **know how to play single notes properly** before purchasing a guitar to test this out (I have lessons on this). Assuming you know how to play single notes, just play random notes all over the fretboard and **let each note sustain** for a few seconds each. Do you hear buzz? Are the notes clear? Try higher notes, try lower notes.

A little bit of buzz is totally ok, especially on an electric. In fact, many electrics are buzzy on their own but the buzz is inaudible when plugged into an amp. Acoustics you have to be a little more careful. How much is too much buzz? Are the notes buzzy the entire time you hold the note?

When purchasing a guitar, you want to find something that just feels easy. Try some chords and songs. What you'll notice is some guitars are just easier to play than others.

For a total beginner that doesn't know how to play too much remember **the eyeball test** of checking out the action of the guitar and 2nd, **the listening test** for buzzy notes. These are 2 of the most important things in buying a guitar. These will make the biggest difference in learning the guitar and making you sound the best you can be.

EPILOGUE

CHAPTER 32

FINAL LESSON! OVERVIEW & WILL'S ADVICE FOR YOU

Epilogue

Congratulations for reaching the end of this course! We have come a long way. This was specially designed to give you the fastest and best way to get from a complete beginner, to someone who can pick up the guitar and play almost any song.

Now the most important thing, the icing on the cake when playing guitar, is to connect with the vibe of the song. If there is one thing I want you to take away from this course it is this...

This is going to be a part of your practice that's **just as important** as your scales and your songs. You picked up the guitar for a reason, that reason is the feeling that music gives us. You now have an instrument and the knowledge to start creating that magic for yourself and others. In order to do this, you need to play with 'feeling' and 'conviction'.

Music and songs are emotional expressions. When you play "Iron Man" or "Seven Nation Army", the more of that futuristic "barbarian" sound you can portray, the better the song will come across. Thinking now about the MGMT song "Kids", try to capture that nostalgic, upbeat, dance vibe. "Leaving on a Jet Plane" has an open heart feel that sounds honest and sad. You need to project that special, unique energy in every song you play.

Understanding the difference between just strumming the right chords and actually connecting with the emotion and translating the vibe is what separates an average guitar player from a great guitar player.

Thank you for supporting my mission, and my chief aim which is to provide the most powerful resources for people who dream of playing the guitar.

If this book has helped you at all, great. If you got access to the video's as well as used this book as a reference point, awesome!

In case that you're still just not "getting it" or are feeling challenged by certain aspects of guitar playing, I'm here to help. You see, every person has a particular way that they learn best. In my experience teaching guitar for many years and from my own personal experience, 1-on-1 lessons is the best and fastest way to learn the guitar.

If you haven't invested your time and money into 1-on-1 lessons yet, I would suggest you do so! My team at http://www.CampfireGuitarStar.com are here to help you with this and support you in your musical goals!

Keep on rippin' it up!

Will Ripley

CAMPFIRE GUITAR STAR

Produced By PATON STUDIOS